Robert Frost: A Pictorial Chronicle

In Memory of Lawrance Thompson

who has left readers and students alike in his debt for his *Selected Letters of Robert Frost* and the two volumes of biography which he lived to complete. While Larry was working on these volumes, we shared information and spent many hours discussing Robert and the episodes of his life that he repeatedly told us both, not always in identical detail. In our exchange of views, Larry and I did not invariably reach the same judgments, but differences of emphasis or interpretation did not impair or limit our friendship. His loss is great.

— K.M.

Published simultaneously in Canada
by Holt, Rinehart and Winston of Canada, Limited
First Edition
Library of Congress Cataloging in Publication Data
Morrison, Kathleen, 1898–
Robert Frost: A pictorial chronicle.

1. Frost, Robert, 1874–1963—Biography.   2. Frost,
Robert, 1874–1963—Portraits, etc.
PS3511.R94Z795   811'.5'2 [B]   74-3383
ISBN 0-03-012601-0

Printed in the United States of America

Acknowledgment is made to Holt, Rinehart and Winston, Inc., and the Estate of Robert Frost for permission to reprint excerpts from the following books:

From *The Poetry of Robert Frost* edited by Edward Connery Lathem. Copyright 1934, 1947, © 1969 by Holt, Rinehart and Winston, Inc. Copyright 1936, 1942, 1947, © 1962 by Robert Frost. Copyright © 1964, 1970 by Lesley Frost Ballantine. From *Selected Letters of Robert Frost* edited by Lawrance Thompson. Copyright © 1964 by Holt, Rinehart and Winston, Inc. From *Interviews with Robert Frost* edited by Edward Connery Lathem. Copyright © 1966 by Holt, Rinehart and Winston, Inc. From *Robert Frost: Poetry and Prose* edited by Edward Connery Lathem and Lawrance Thompson. Copyright © 1972 by Holt, Rinehart and Winston, Inc. From *The Letters of Robert Frost to Louis Untermeyer.* Copyright © 1963 by Holt, Rinehart and Winston, Inc. From *Robert Frost and John Bartlett* by Margaret Bartlett Anderson. Copyright © 1963 by Margaret Bartlett Anderson.

ROBERT
FROST

A

PICTORIAL

CHRONICLE

KATHLEEN   MORRISON

HOLT, RINEHART AND WINSTON   NEW YORK CHICAGO SAN FRANCISCO

Acknowledgments

For whatever I have accomplished in this chronicle, I first owe thanks to my husband, Theodore Morrison, who bore with housekeeping neglect and interruptions to his own work all the while giving me encouragement and reminding me of the possibilities of the English sentence. I also thank my daughter, Anne Morrison Smyth, not only for interest in the manuscript but also for years of devoted attention to Robert Frost. To Elizabeth Perkins Aldrich more than conventional appreciation is due for her early and continuing support and for her final reading of the pages with a fresh eye and fastidious taste. Without Alfred C. Edwards in his role as president of Holt, Rinehart, and Winston, Inc., as Trustee of the Robert Frost Estate, and as a staunch friend, I could not have finished what I intended. He has also generously allowed me to quote from the unpublished notebooks of Robert Frost.

No words could possibly express my thanks to Edward Connery Lathem, long-time friend and Dean of Libraries at Dartmouth College. He has anticipated my every need and willingly shared with me the resources of Dartmouth College, as well as his own valuable advice. Cordial thanks are also due to members of his staff—Adelaide Lockhart, Director of Library Services; Kenneth Cramer in charge of the archives; and Claire Packard, executive secretary. I gladly acknowledge my debt to Sue Marcoulier, for the past months my research assistant and now a librarian in the new Kresge Library at Dartmouth. I am grateful to all those photographers and film makers who in the course of their duties found time to be thoughtful of me in my somewhat precarious position between not always harmonious forces.

Finally, I cannot forget those many friends of Robert Frost without whose generous help I could not have survived. It is with gratitude that I further acknowledge the generosity of the following libraries which allowed me to use their resources: the Amherst College Library, the Dartmouth College Library, the Houghton Library at Harvard, the Jones Library at Amherst, the Library of Congress, and the Middlebury College Library.

I am grateful for photographs from the Amherst College News Service; the Embassy of Israel, Washington, D.C.; the Hebrew Institute, New York; the Herbert H. Lamson Library at Plymouth State College,

Plymouth, New Hampshire; the Middlebury College News Bureau; the National Archives and Records Service, Washington, D.C.; and the National Park Service, Washington, D.C.

To the following friends I am indebted for the use of their photographs: Bernard Cannon, Corinne Tennyson Davids, Avis DeVoto, Jarvis Mason, Franklin Reeve, David Rhinelander, and Lois Tilley Lewis.

To Holt, Rinehart and Winston, Inc., I owe permission to quote excerpts from *The Poetry of Robert Frost,* from *Selected Letters* edited by Lawrance Thompson, from *The Letters of Robert Frost to Louis Untermeyer,* from *Robert Frost and John Bartlett* by Margaret Bartlett Anderson, from *Interviews with Robert Frost* edited by Edward Connery Lathem, from *Robert Frost, Prose and Poetry* edited by Edward Connery Lathem and Lawrance Thompson, from *Selected Prose of Robert Frost* edited by Hyde Cox and Edward Connery Lathem. The *Concordance to the Poetry of Robert Frost* edited by Edward Connery Lathem has proved an indispensable convenience.

I have also had the generous permission of Franklin Reeve to draw on his book, *Robert Frost in Russia,* and of Frederick B. Adams from his book, *To Russia with Frost.*

$-K.M.$

Contents

Foreword

For almost thirty years I kept a vow to myself not to write about Robert Frost. In fact I rejected overtures from publishers who thought that because of my close association with Frost—virtually as his manager in his later years—I might commit myself to paper. Then some years ago it occurred to me that a pictorial biography of this marvelously photogenic subject ought to exist. I had a wealth of illustrations on my hands, and I thought first of a book that, for text, would need hardly more than explanatory captions. Then I began to see that I was privileged by circumstances to relate these pictures to Frost's life in a way that must necessarily go beyond the range of captions. The present book is thus the result of a balance between the claims of pictures and the claims of text. The book concentrates on the three decades during which I was in close association with Frost, but it attempts by flashbacks and other means to give at least an outline of his whole life, as a reminder—hopefully from a fresh point of view—to those who already know his story and as an introduction to those not familiar with it.

No photograph, however good, could possibly do justice to some of the qualities that marked Robert as a very unusual man—his brilliant conversation, for example, or the remarkable mind that could cut through trivialities and come up with a deep understanding of matters not ordinarily considered within the scope of poetry. At home as a devoted amateur in astronomy, archaeology, history, botany, he astounded scientists by his ready understanding of underlying principles even in areas as recondite as mathematics and nuclear fission. This formidable mind—constantly active, skeptical, believing, joking, probing, mocking, sometimes giving offense, sometimes warmly genial, the delight and wonder of visitors from everywhere—underlies every picture and is the despair of anyone who tries to capture it in words. But words are necessary. A strictly pictorial biography must accept the limitations of the pictures available; gaps are inevitable in even the fullest photographic record. After all, it wasn't on every occasion in Frost's life that photographers were present. Also, photographs vary in technical excellence as well as in suitability for reproduction. I have tried to keep the pictorial record as representative as possible; where it fails I have resorted to words in an effort to redress the imbalance as well as I could by text.

I

Depths Below Depths

"And I the last go forth companionless"

In 1938, after the sudden death from heart failure of his wife, Elinor, in Gainesville, Florida, Robert Frost was described by his poet-novelist friend, Hervey Allen, as "a great and powerful engine without the control of its flywheel." The description was just. The disruption of his marriage after forty-three years was a blow too heavy to take. From the year 1892, when he and Elinor White had shared honors as valedictorians at their graduation from high school in Lawrence, Massachusetts, she had been his love and his refuge. The courtship had been stormy. One of its climactic episodes occurred when Robert found himself unable to accept Elinor's decision that their formal marriage must wait until he had become established in a career and she had earned her college degree. He paid an unannounced visit to her at St. Lawrence University in Canton, New York, where she was studying. He carried with him the only two copies of a privately printed little book, *Twilight,* containing four new poems in addition to "My Butterfly," his first poem to be accepted for publication by a national magazine, *The Independent.* Elinor refused to admit him to the private house where she boarded. Leaving one copy of *Twilight* with her, he turned away, and as he walked to the railroad station tore up his own copy, scattering the pieces along the track. Once home in Lawrence, unable to listen to the explanations Elinor's mother must have given him and unable to realize that there might have been regulations governing the presence of men in an all-female building, he took off for Norfolk, Virginia, intent on finding the Dismal Swamp. I don't believe that anyone has ever discovered how he knew about the Dismal Swamp, but he thought of it as the possible place where he might end his life and so mete out the proper punishment to Elinor, who had so obviously forgotten their vows of eternal love and their exchange of gold wedding rings in the summer of 1892. To my knowledge this is the first of many threats to punish those opposing his wishes by making them sorry for his death —an evidence of that deeply hidden sense of insecurity that dogged him to the end of his life, even in his final days of triumph.

In spite of stresses and strains, his had been a marriage that rested on a true and deep bond, a marriage that made the poetry possible. Elinor had provided judgment, encouragement, and the necessary faith in him as a poet. In her early photographs one sees great beauty in a somewhat serious face; in her later pictures one detects sadness and a growing austerity, as if life had taken too heavy a toll. One needs only to look at the poems to see the depth of their tie, as in these lines from "Flower-Gathering":

> I left you in the morning,
> And in the morning glow
> You walked a way beside me
> To make me sad to go.

Depths Below Depths

When asked, "How did you become a poet?" R.F. answered, "I followed the procession down the ages."

(Blackington, Boston, Dartmouth College Archives)

Or in a stanza from "In Neglect":

> They leave us so to the way we took,
>   As two in whom they were proved mistaken,
> That we sit sometimes in the wayside nook,
> With mischievous, vagrant, seraphic look,
>   And *try* if we cannot feel forsaken.

It was no wonder that after his wife's death Robert was constantly troubled by opposing emotions—rebellion and acceptance, self-accusation and self-justification, dependence and wilfullness. Lawrance Thompson, in a painstakingly true and profoundly touching passage in the second volume of his Frost biography, describes how Robert paced the corridor outside the upstairs room in Gainesville where Elinor lay dying of successive heart attacks, hoping to be admitted and to gain from her some word or look of assurance that the marriage had been worth its cost. He was not admitted and never received the longed for message. Word has somehow spread that Elinor refused to let him enter. Whether this legend comes from a misreading of Thompson or from reviews of his book that relished the chance to pounce on Robert's vulnerabilities, it overlooks the facts. Elinor was too near death to give or withhold. It would have been the doctor who refused en-

6

trance, knowing that Robert would have been unable to control his emotions and might well hasten the death he dreaded. When death occurred, Robert blamed himself unmercifully, believing that he had asked too much of her because of his own selfishness. Wounded by the accusations of his daughter Lesley that he had done great injury to his children and that he was the kind of artist who should never have married, he succumbed to a throat infection and within days was in a state of complete collapse, physical and emotional. On April 12 he was able to write to his old friend, Hervey Allen, quoting Tennyson:

> And I the last go forth companionless
> And the days darken round me . . .

But on the same day he wrote to Bernard DeVoto: "I expect to have to go to depths below depths in thinking before I catch myself and can say what I want to while I last. I shall be all right in public, but I can't tell you how I am going to behave when I am alone."

It was more than days, more than months, even years, before he reconciled himself to the universe, to those powers that had brought down on his head such unexpected misfortune. "I never thought this would be done to me" was his constant cry. He was not "right in public," nor could he anticipate the extremes of his behavior in private. He spent money recklessly. In a symbolic revolt against the limited circumstances in which he and Elinor had lived, and delighting in the thought of the pleasure small boys would have in picking them up, he threw pennies and loose change of every denomination into school-yards and on to the streets. Trying to prove himself "a bad, bad man," he laced his conversation with innuendos of sexual exploits that were utterly foreign to his nature, laughable in view of his confession that when he traveled in a train he would abandon his lower berth for the smoking car should a woman be the occupant of the upper. From some-one who had never cared for alcohol he became the great experimenter. Unsophisticated in the use of stimulants, he would try exotic liqueurs and would mix unfriendly ingredients. Luckily his head was strong. In spite of all his efforts he failed to impress his friends as a devil of a fellow. In much the same way in these years after Elinor's death, and in later years also, he used medicine not solely as a cure but as a power-ful threat, a way of asserting himself. His incautious use of pills always stopped short of the ultimate message it was meant to convey. Like a child he learned that his threats did not succeed, but he never gave up trying.

After the blow that had left him so distraught, Robert had to make some plan for his life, and his natural thought was to divide his time among his children. At South Shaftsbury in Vermont he had acquired the beautiful Stone House, as it was called, where his only surviving son Carol and his daughter-in-law Lillian were living, Carol tending an apple orchard that Robert had enabled him to set out. Here Robert meant to retreat for the early months of spring and summer; or, if arrangements at the Stone House proved unsuccessful, he owned an equally beautiful house, the Gulley, standing across the highway and up a steep hill. Later in the summer he would move to Concord Corners—an almost abandoned village near St. Johnsbury in northern Vermont—where in 1936 he had bought two houses, both in need of repair. They looked out over a pond and toward a view of the New Hampshire mountains, and gave Robert the pleasure he always took in attractively situated farms and in houses that could be saved or improved by judicious alteration. He found further interest in Concord Corners because it was there, he learned, that Samuel Read Hall had established the first Normal School for the training of teachers. In a letter to his friend Harold Goddard Rugg at Dartmouth College he wrote: "This is a strange place for me to have landed in by luck. It looks as if fate wanted to reconcile me to pedagogy. It will be the last

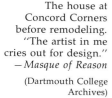

The house at Concord Corners before remodeling. "The artist in me cries out for design." —*Masque of Reason*

(Dartmouth College Archives)

surrender. I have been a long time making my peace with the academic, but I can't be said not to have made it in full." Robert had originally meant Concord Corners to provide a nook of escape for himself and for Elinor during the season of hay fever, to which he was extremely susceptible. It turned out also to be a place where his daughter Irma and her husband John Cone could find a respite from city pressures, and where John could use his architectural skill by restoring the houses. It was to Concord Corners that Robert expected to make his August escape from the affliction he dreaded. Winters, he thought, would pose no problem. He could spend some time with his eldest daughter, Lesley Frost Francis, and her two daughters in Washington, where Lesley had become Assistant Director of the King-Smith Studio School, and after that he could go as usual to Florida.

But events did not turn out the way he expected. As time passed he was forced to reconsider the feasibility of staying for extended periods with his children. He did not "wander around them for a while," as he wrote to his old friend Roy Elliott, "until I can decide what I am now, and what I have to go on with." For two months he tried to fill his days working with Carol at the Stone House farm in South Shaftsbury, taking long walks, botanizing as he used to do, but always returning tired and lonely, a rare orchis in hand, to find no one there to know it as

> The measure of the little while
> That I've been long away.

He reached the belief that his presence was not good for Carol, whose own problems were only intensified by Robert's consistent conviction that he knew how to direct other people's lives. He did not accept the proposal Carol and Lillian made that he could build an ell on the Stone

R.F. with Gillie at Dartmouth. "What we do in college is to get over our little-mindedness."

(Eric Schaal, Life Magazine © Time Inc.)

House for his own use. He realized also that life with Lesley would not be possible. The breach between them that had occurred immediately after Elinor's death was an example of their difficulties with each other. Lesley and her father were too much alike, with the same virtues, the same faults. Though two people never talked more easily together, sharing the same intellectual interests, the same devotion and concern for family matters, their great pride in each other did not prevent torrential clashes. Life at Concord Corners offered no better prospect than life at South Shaftsbury or in Washington. Irma was not well, showing signs of the psychiatric disorder that later became acute and carrying the same resentments against her father that had made the breach with Lesley. In a letter to Mary Goodwillie, a close family friend of long standing, he summed up himself and his situation and recorded a deci-

9

sion he had reached in June of 1938, three months after Elinor's death: "I have been running pretty wild and irresponsible the last few months. . . . I have given up Amherst and given up the idea of settling down with any of the children. Luckily things are fine for at least two of them and if none too happy for the third [Irma] surely beyond my personal powers to make any happier. I am filling my immediate future full of lectures and distractions and propose to go it till I almost drop."

Robert's reference to giving up Amherst represents an important break he made in the course of deciding to "go it alone," a break that marked, not for the first time, his way of seeking "freedom in departure." Ever since 1917, with certain interruptions, Amherst College had given him an important source of income and a forum where he could meet with students and bring them under the spell of his utterly unconventional but fertile gifts as a teacher, an interlocutor, a purveyor of ideas. Three times he had been tempted away to the University of Michigan at Ann Arbor, where he hoped for freedom to write uninterrupted by the demands of academic life and by the unavoidable frictions of an academic community. Some of the frictions he felt at Amherst sprang from ideas and practices of President Alexander Meiklejohn to which Robert was antipathetic. He was repelled in particular by the mores of some of the men President Meiklejohn appointed to faculty positions. But Michigan did not reward him with his kind of freedom, and so in 1926 he returned to Amherst. In the year of Elinor's death, she and Robert owned a fine Victorian house at 15 Sunset Avenue, their seventh residence in the town since Robert's first connection with the college. After a break with President Stanley King, in which the understanding and the generosity of spirit of which Robert was capable did not show to advantage, he sold the house and cut his ties with an institution that had given him important opportunities, though in later years he was to renew his links with it. His decision to leave Amherst was not entirely unexpected. Some faculty members resented the freedom from formal teaching that he enjoyed. Some had complained that he was not living up to the terms of his contract with President King. Others felt that his bringing friends such as Louis Untermeyer or Amy Lowell to read or lecture drained Amherst funds unfairly. The result of all these circumstances was that in June 1938 Robert found himself bereft, without a home, with no prospect of living with his children, and with no academic ties.

It was at this juncture that he remembered an invitation my husband and I had given him after the memorial service for Elinor in Johnson Chapel at Amherst. We told him that he was welcome to stay with us in Cambridge whenever he felt the need of housing or company in the city. This invitation had important effects both for us and for Robert. In any case it is important enough to the story of our relations with him so that its roots need to be understood. To trace those roots adequately it is necessary to go back through the years to 1918, when I was a student at Bryn Mawr College.

"I'm not confused, I'm just well mixed."
(David Rhinelander)

10

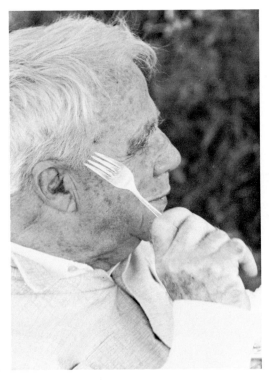

At that time a number of us at Bryn Mawr who were interested in the reading and writing of poetry decided we wanted to bring to the campus a poet who would sit with us, talk with us, and perhaps give a public lecture. We chose Robert Frost, fresh home from publication and recognition in England and currently teaching at Amherst. We knew that we would have to raise the money for his fee ourselves; the college could not afford it. After collecting almost five hundred dollars and making our plans with Mr. Frost, we called on President M. Carey Thomas to inform her of our *fait accompli.* Somewhat taken aback, she soon forgave us our presumption and after a few moments showed her pleasure at our initiative. Perhaps we might be bringing to the college a young poet whose later fame would bring as much kudos to Bryn Mawr as her own somewhat ruthlessly gained appointments of

"I like the actuality of gossip, the intimacy of it."

(David Rhinelander)

Woodrow Wilson and Jacques Loeb. With money in hand and official permission given we were on our way. Robert came four times in the ensuing year, and in the year following gave a lecture open to the college and to the community. Our group, calling ourselves "The Reelers and Writhers" printed three booklets with the title *The Humble Voyagers.* One of our members was Jean Flexner, whose writing Robert thought highly of; she, with his Amherst pupil, Carter Goodrich, was the subject of his poem "The Lost Follower."

After I graduated from Bryn Mawr and studied for a year at Oxford, I saw little of Robert until March 1936. At that time he came to Harvard University to deliver six lectures on the Charles Eliot Norton Foundation. My husband, Theodore Morrison, and I, with our six-year-old son, were living on Mason Street in Cambridge in a four-family brick house, vertically divided. Our immediate neighbors, who had found us this Victorian refuge during the trough of the Great Depression, were Bernard DeVoto and his wife Avis. He and my husband were fellow members of the English Department at Harvard. Avis, of Scottish descent and Midwestern upbringing, was an outspoken critic of sham and complacency. These were lively days on the Harvard scene. Leverett House, where my husband was a tutor, was dubbed "Moscow on the Charles." Faculty wives flaunted banners in favor of striking Yellow Taxicab drivers. Over teacups on Friday afternoons in the Leverett House drawing room, men and women outdid one another in pedantic disputes over facts and dates. In literary circles it was a time of coteries with political overtones. Harvard had its New Deal liberals and its closely organized communist sympathizers as well as its natural share of conservatives.

The invitation to give the Norton Lectures reached Robert in Florida, where he was making his regular retreat from northern winters and their accompanying bouts of pneumonia. He had hesitations about accepting the offer. He dreaded the necessity of writing out the lectures for publication by the Harvard University Press, and never did fulfill this part of his contract. He feared that in Cambridge he would find fewer friends than enemies, remembering how those he labeled radicals had reacted to his poem "Build Soil," which he had read four years earlier at Columbia University. He dreaded facing what he called the "Pro-English" faction in the Harvard community. By "Pro-English" he really meant the more partisan admirers of his predecessor in the Norton lectureship, T. S. Eliot. He knew he had strong supporters in David McCord; in Robert Hillyer; in Arthur Stanley Pease, who had come to the Harvard Classics Department from Amherst; in his old friend F.N. Robinson, Chaucerian scholar who also had his roots in Lawrence, Massachusetts; and in his newly-made friend, Bernard DeVoto. In spite of his fears he accepted the lectureship, thus returning to the college he had left in 1899 during his second year as a special student. He had left Dartmouth even more prematurely seven years earlier. Perhaps these two further examples of finding "freedom in departure" helped give him the courage to face his talks for the Norton Foundation, talks he was to call "The Renewal of Words."

Official arrangements for entertaining the Frosts were skimpy at best. It fell to Avis DeVoto and me to find them the house that the Norton Committee had assured them would be provided. After diligent search we found a furnished house on Fayerweather Street where they could ensconce themselves in reasonable comfort. Although my husband was still in the junior teaching ranks of the University, Ted and I were able to offer Robert evening hospitality and the conversation of our friends after five of his six lectures. We had not been able to discover that any arrangements had been made for entertaining Robert after his lectures. It was then we had our first experience of providing the private snack of sandwiches, salad, or cold meat that Robert always needed after going supperless to his public performance. Elinor Frost celebrated the conclusion of the series with a party on Fayerweather Street. A bad cold had housed her for the first weeks, but even in the succeeding ones she followed her established pattern of not going to the lecture but waiting up eagerly at home to hear how it had been received. Perhaps her custom of not listening to Robert's talks had its roots in her wish to keep him as "her poet" and not a public performer. Perhaps she knew how deeply she might hurt him if she showed the slightest hint of criticism. Robert never did definitely state his view of her habitual absence from his readings. He took refuge in a phrase I have heard him call on often and on many varied occasions when he felt the need of reticence: "It was thought best . . ."

These six evenings after the Norton Lectures confirmed and strengthened what I had earlier suspected in my days at Bryn Mawr, namely, that to encounter Robert Frost was to encounter one of the notable minds of a generation, a mind with restless curiosity seeking for the truth unfettered by second-hand opinions and moving to its target swiftly as an arrow. Many witnesses could testify to the range of his intellectual force. In his "Education by Poetry," a talk given before the Amherst College Alumni Council in 1930, he drew analogies from science prompted by a conversation at a dinner party given by President George Olds to honor the Danish atomic physicist, Niels Bohr. It was later said of this dinner party that Robert asked Mr. Bohr questions more penetrating than those of professional scientists. I was later a witness to a similar interchange with Harvey Brooks, Dean of Engineering and Applied Physics at Harvard, an interchange that took place shortly after the publication of the Smyth Report, the earliest official public account of the process underlying the atomic bomb. Robert impressed and surprised his scientific friend with his intuitive understanding of the principles involved. When he became a member of the Saturday Club, a group of eminent men in many branches of learning and the professions who lunched once a month at the Union Club in Boston, Robert held his own with such fellow members as Harlow Shapley, the astronomer, Charles P. Curtis, the lawyer and co-editor of *The Practical Cogitator*, John Finley, Professor of Greek Literature, and Felix Frankfurter, the Justice. Occasionally he piqued these colleagues by riding roughshod over their systematically argued views with his conversational brilliance and wit.

It was the series of evenings after the Norton Lectures, representing for me a renewal of the friendship begun at Bryn Mawr, that made possible the invitation my husband and I extended to Robert after his bereavement, offering him our house in Cambridge as a refuge when he might need it. His first response caught us in a dilemma. Ted supplemented his Harvard income by teaching in Vermont at the Bread Loaf Summer School of English and by directing the Bread Loaf Writers' Conference, both sponsored by Middlebury

R.F. and
Anne Morrison in
1938 at Bread Loaf.
"Never give a
child a choice.
Don't give him
a chance of be-
lieving in God
or not. He can
start having
choices when he
goes to college."

(Bernard De Voto)

College and housed in Bread Loaf Inn and its surrounding cottages.
The successive terms of the School and the Conference ran from late
June until just before the Labor Day weekend. During that crucial
month of June in 1938, when Robert was at his most footloose and disconsolate, Ted and I were packed and ready for our exodus to Vermont
with our two children when Robert surprised us by a telephone call
from the St. Botolph Club in Boston, saying: "I'm here as you asked."
We explained our predicament. Robert immediately saw our problems,
and I in turn began to think of ways by which we might be of help
to him during the summer.

Bread Loaf was and is a remarkable place and institution. The Inn
is a spreading, four-story, wooden Victorian structure, perhaps not
large enough to be called immense but sufficiently impressive in size.
Across the road from it stand houses and cottages of varying degrees
of pretension, but also Victorian. Behind it trail the Little Theater
and lecture hall, and behind that the library, beside three tennis
courts. Still farther to the rear, beyond an extensive meadow where a
fine herd of cows once pastured, rises the barn, an imposing square

15

Depths Below Depths

At Bread Loaf.
(1) "My life
was a risk
I had to take—
and took."
(2) R. F., Archibald MacLeish,
Theodore
Morrison, 1938.

(Bernard
De Voto)

(3) Session
with students.

(Dartmouth
College
Archives)

edifice topped by a mansard roof. Ample open fields merge southward and eastward into the folds and crests of the Green Mountains, covered as far as eye can see by the hardwood stands, the spruces and hemlocks and balsams, of the National Forest which clothes so much of mountain Vermont. Bread Loaf lies within the village of Ripton, and the Bread Loaf property was left to Middlebury College by Joseph Battell, a benevolent eccentric, keeper for years of the Morgan horse stallion register and author of such unconventional pseudo-philosophic works as *Ellen, or the Whisperings of an Old Pine.* Faced with the problem of what to do with such a bequest, Middlebury decided to use it as the mountain campus for a summer school of English studies, a supplement to the foreign language schools for which the College had made itself internationally known. The Writers' Conference, the pioneer of such enterprises, was added for the economic purpose of keeping the staff together for the normal eight-week period of summer employment, but Robert himself was a participant in the discussions that led to its inaugural session in 1926. After a difference with its early director, John Farrar, Robert lent his presence only intermittently to the Conference until, with some difficulty, my husband lured him back in 1935.

To an outsider it might seem that Bread Loaf offered a favorable terrain for children. It had outdoor games, acres of woods in which to walk or explore nature, trout streams in which to fish. Deer, rabbits, and foxes could be seen frequently, and on rare occasions there was the chance of meeting a bear or a wildcat. But in 1938 some sort of tradition of academic austerity excluded children from residence, a restriction since happily remedied. I could find no nearby cottage to rent, and so I had planned to take our eight-year-old son and eighteen-month-old daughter to board with the Nathaniel Sages, friends in West Dover, Vermont, where young people would be available to take care of the children whenever it might be possible for me to join Ted at Bread Loaf. In the the course of Robert's unexpected June telephone call from the St. Botolph Club, I had invited him to visit at West Dover, as he did on two occasions. There he became acquainted with the Sages and their daughters, one of whom, familiarly called Bunty, later spent four happy summers with us after I finally found (in 1939) a house conveniently near Bread Loaf for family living during the School and Conference season, the Homer Noble Farm in Ripton. Robert also came to know the Sages' family retainer, "Ma Jenks," Mrs. Mary Jenkins, who in 1940 became our housekeeper. I had also ended my telephone conversation with him on that evening in 1938 with the promise that when he came as a staff member to the Writers' Conference in August, he could count on us for companionship and care, he in one of the Inn cottages and we as a family in a house loaned to us by Mr. Endicott, one of the regular Bread Loaf colonists.

In August the Conference gathered as usual for its two weeks of intensive lecturing and criticism. Never an easy fortnight, this session outdid others in the problems it presented. In the house that had been provided for us off campus, Ted and I were somewhat protected from the hourly problems, but the daily ones accumulated. Robert was lodged in a faculty cottage shared by those we knew were aware of his state and who would watch over his comings and goings and his late risings. He was still not "right" in public. His talks were larded with unfounded allusions to his own "badness" and to behavior not proven by fact. All this accompanied the wit and wisdom of his usual Bread Loaf talks. Leisure time brought up other problems. Bernard DeVoto, Herschel Brickell, Robeson Bailey, and their wives conspired to walk with him, talk with him, and supply his late-breakfast needs of a raw egg and milk diluted with coffee. Couples played endless sets of doubles tennis, doggedly fought and exhausting to Robert's partner, whose life depended on no double faults and no missed balls. His moods were unpredictable. Brilliant talk before the

Village Street, Ripton, Vermont.

At Ripton. (1) R.F. and K.M. leaving the cabin after a morning's work.

(Jacob Lofman)

(2) The Homer Noble team and sleigh during a Christmas visit.

wood fire of an evening at the faculty cottage often ended in abrupt departure, leaving his colleagues uncertain of the true reason — perhaps a distasteful argument or a fancied slight; more often the need for a solitary five-mile walk on the road toward the mountains. There were days when our old Plymouth bumped its way over every narrow dirt road in the nearby hills as I drove Robert in search of new sights, perhaps an abandoned farmhouse, but more likely a flock of sheep nibbling the scant browse of a rocky pasture. The sheep were there to confirm Robert's belief that a man who cared enough could make a go of it even on five scraggly acres. Didn't he have a well-thumbed book on his shelves called *Five Acres and Independence*?

Early in the session Robert demanded instant transportation to Concord Corners to visit his daughter Irma and her architect husband, John Cone. Normally the remodeling of the houses that John was carrying out would have fascinated him, and he would have more than matched the trained eye of his son-in-law by his amazing ability to plan in his head without benefit of paper or board and to indicate where the two-foot pine boards already in the house would show to better advantage. But not this time. Enraged because Irma put him in a room with no entrance or exit except through the master bedroom, and because she said she would gladly have him stay with them but would accept none of his friends, he sent for Herschel Brickell to drive him back to Bread Loaf.

The session ended and Robert joined us at the Endicott cottage, where Ted and I planned to stay until the opening of the Harvard term. Robert was obviously in need of someone to pull his life together and manage his affairs. He persuaded me to give up the part-time job I had at the time as a reader at the Atlantic Monthly Press and Little, Brown and Company, and instead to take him on permanently,

acting as a kind of managing secretary. As I look back I wonder how I had the temerity to agree. But for one thing, it was the kind of challenge I liked. For another, my friendship with him, despite his current state, had been an easy one, the kind that smoothly falls into place. It had progressed from my young days at Bryn Mawr through the evenings after the Norton Lectures, then through a conversation in the following year at the Boston Book Fair when he told me of Elinor's operation for cancer and the terrible dread it brought him, and so on to our meeting after the service in Johnson Chapel. To take on the proffered work seemed like a continuation of a friendship already established. As I look back, I realize also that Robert's plea tied in with my relationship with my father and his friends, by whom I had been treated almost as an equal and had been admired and affectionately accepted as one of their circle. My father had recently died, and in a way the job Robert invited me to take came as something to make up for the loss. Perhaps I was naive. My father had been a difficult person, but the man I was undertaking to manage was a thousand times more complicated.

Robert's stay at Endicott was a pleasant one. I had been able to secure a fine household helper. We took drives into the back country. We walked and went on picnics. Robert made friends with our lively eight-year-old son, Bobby, and was especially fond of our eighteen-month-old daughter, Anne. But then the rains came and we all found ourselves housebound and chafing at restraint. Just before the brooks rose and the roads began to wash out, Robert left to stay with friends at Pierson College at Yale where he had been made an Associate and had become an annual visitor. He had been gone a day or two when, with almost no warning, the deadly 1938 hurricane hit the whole Eastern seaboard. Ted and I hastily packed our belongings, the children, and the dog in our Plymouth and started for Cambridge. When we finally reached home after an eight-hour drive over half-washed-out detours and through chopped gaps in fallen trees, we found that Robert — distraught, lonely, and worried about his children — had traveled by taxi from ravaged Saybrook to the St. Botolph Club in Boston. Learning that the club would not admit women, not even to the parlor, to discuss lecture arrangements, he moved petulantly to the Ritz Hotel. Frustrated there, he wound up in the hospital with a serious cold. After a dispute with his nurse, he dressed and — unless my memory is very wrong — walked out undismissed, true to his own words: "I've lived a life of decisions, not indecisions, not even consulting anyone."

After Ted and I were settled in Cambridge, I began looking for quarters for Robert. With the help of friends I found an apartment at 88 Mt. Vernon Street in Boston, opposite Louisburg Square. By mid-October his furniture had been brought from storage at Amherst and he was established. In my new secretarial and managerial capacity the understanding was that I should go from Cambridge to Boston around half past nine in the morning and supposedly leave at four in the afternoon. But from the time I first began to work with him until the end, time was of no consequence. I could be summoned after hours, on Saturdays and Sundays, on holidays, sometimes finding real problems but more often emotional upsets. For three years Mt. Vernon Street, with a shift from a front to a more attractive side apartment, proved adequate, but by 1941 it was obvious that Robert needed more space in which to move around. He needed stairs to climb, his own door to lock and open, and quiet streets on which he could take night walks accompanied by Gillie, his Border collie. Gillie, a grandson of the international champion "Old Meg," had been raised in Martha's Vineyard. He was of Scottish descent, and true to his Highland name proved a loyal servant-companion to his master. Seldom were they separated until Gillie's death.

Away from Boston, Robert might miss encounters such as he had one New Year's Day when, walking around the less elegant side of Beacon Hill, he brushed off the incoherent advances of a drunk and was rudely asked: "Who do you think you are—the late George Apley?" But he would be more protected. After a search I came on a three-story Victorian house at 35 Brewster Street in Cambridge. He bought it, and from there as headquarters in what was locally known as "Brewster Village" he started his new life, which he liked to describe as "barding around the country."

Summers presented other problems. In 1939 Ted and I rented the Homer Noble Farm in Ripton from the widowed owner, Mrs. Noble. The farm, near enough to Bread Loaf for Ted's summer teaching and directing, was a substantial one of about one hundred and fifty acres or more, part pasture, part woodland, and bounded on three sides by the Green Mountain National Forest. Originally the owners raised cattle and sheep and sold their own maple syrup. Their only source of power was a windmill near the barn. After Mr. Noble's death, the farm survived mainly on the income from summer and hunting-season boarders, from sugar-on-snow parties for the students of Middlebury College, and from the rent of a three-room cabin built by Mrs. Noble's

The house at 35 Brewster Street, Cambridge.

(From *"A Lover's Quarrel with the World"*)

21

The
Homer Noble
Farm.
(1) In 1939.
(2) Painted
and with
the addition
of an ell de-
signed by R.F.

(Bernard M.
Cannon)

adopted son, Harold Whittemore. In 1939 this cabin was occupied by students from the Bread Loaf School of English and so was unavailable for Robert's use. I found a small house for him in Ripton Hollow opposite one owned by Miss Agnes Billings, town clerk and sister of Mrs. Noble. These two ladies took boarders and there Robert had meals seldom equaled.

Sometime in August Mrs. Noble decided to sell, and she put the Homer Noble Farm on the market. Robert proposed that he buy it, lease the main house to us, and live during the summer season in the cabin some two hundred or more yards to the north. He outlined a scheme of operation. We would pay him the same rent as we paid Mrs. Noble. We would maintain the interior of the farm house—paint, paper, and appliances—and would employ necessary household help. He would pay his share of food costs, maintain the outside premises, and

R.F. as a boarder at the home of Agnes Billings in Ripton, with Mrs. Homer Noble on his right and Professor Ray Nash on Miss Billings' left.

(Eric Schaal, Life Magazine © Time Inc.)

hire a man to farm. In turn we would provide his meals, a basket lunch at the cabin and supper at the farmhouse. At supper his friends would be welcome as well as our own. Not without trepidation and some reluctance, we agreed to his proposal. Ted and I could not at that time afford to buy the place. No other houses within striking distance of Bread Loaf were available for us to rent. And whatever apprehensions we felt, the situation would be ideal for our children. They could swim, fish, learn about rabbits, raccoons, deer, and harmless snakes— our son even had an unsupervised confrontation with a bear—and all this without the organized formalities of camp life. We anticipated complications and difficulties, but by the time August saw the closing of Bread Loaf everything had been settled. The farm had been bought and a course laid out for future summers, a course by no means straight and easy, but with a promise of rewards to match its often taxing demands.

23

II

The Academic Farmer

*"My favorite implements (after the pen)
are the axe and the scythe"*

As far back as April 1915 his English poet-friend, Edward Thomas, had written to Robert, who was then farming in Franconia, New Hampshire: "I hope people aren't going to crowd to see you milking and find out whether your private life is also like a page from Theocritus." No hope could have better fitted the Homer Noble Farm in the summers of 1940 and in the years following, for Robert had occasion many a time to try to circumvent the stream of visitors waiting to invade his privacy.

The days moved in a rigidly divided pattern. From ten in the morning until three in the afternoon Robert's life was his own, a time when he might write, read, or merely think. During these hours I was the only presence allowed in the cabin with him. Lunch basket in hand, I would climb the hill from the farmhouse, to find him seated in the Morris chair surrounded by notebooks scattered about the floor, sometimes pen in hand and paper on the homemade writing board across his knees, or other days turning the pages of *The Oxford Book of English Verse* or Darwin's account of his voyage on the *Beagle*. His legs would be spread out in front of him, his navy-blue Keds resting on an old newspaper, and a jacket-shirt, blue as his eyes, surmounting a somewhat rumpled white shirt open at the neck. I never knew what to expect. Never a greeting, but instead a continuation of what the day before had brought. Why had his publisher said what he had said? Was his last night's talk at Bread Loaf as misunderstood as he feared? Would I please write to that man in Chicago and say that what had been proposed was not his kind of performance? If I was unfortunate enough to have been delayed by a household crisis below, I would find the cabin empty, his breakfast milk glass by the chair, and the atmosphere a foreshadowing of the storm that would break with his return from the woods some hours later.

During the working hours the farm received only his left-handed attention, if that. But at three, Robert would take to the garden, hoe and spade in hand. He hacked at the weeds; he soothed, cajoled, or gave orders to the current hired man. He wandered, or as one of our local friends described it, "mogged along" in the woods, testing the hollows for underground springs, discovering hidden witch hazel, goldthread, mianthemum, and wild cucumber. Then, as evening came on, Robert would join us for a family supper with the children, often with guests, his, ours, or both. After supper he would take his visitors up to the cabin. Frequently they were friends with whom he delighted to talk till all hours; sometimes they were less eagerly welcomed claimants on his attention. Quiet descended on the farm only late after darkness, when the last voices came down the lane from the cabin, signifying that Robert was putting his night's quota of pilgrims on the dirt road down to the highway. At midnight or beyond Robert's lantern could be seen bobbing up the hill to the cabin again, and the silence of a country night would settle in behind him.

We at the farmhouse were constantly being surprised, never know-

ing quite what to expect. Sometimes returning home late in the evening, ready for bed, we would drive up our road to discover an unidentifiable car resting on the barn ramp with its driver eagerly waiting to catch Robert and present him with still another personal or academic problem. Once we came downstairs to breakfast to find a well-known poet of expansive build asleep on the living room sofa, not alone but sharing its minimal dimensions with a St. Bernard. Talk at the cabin had proved exhausting.

The daily routine was interrupted by shopping trips to Middlebury or drives over the "gap" to Woodstock in search of the jarred goodies, tinned meats, and cheeses that turned the cabin shelves into a storehouse of treats for Robert's discriminating taste and gave him reassurance that his lean days had passed forever. Though delicacies were a chief object of these expeditions, they were not the only one. Robert used to joke that he was an egalitarian, only comfortable in the society of his equals. But he was quick to find common ground with people of all sorts. He made friends with proprietors and clerks in shops; and a butcher who could cut a choice slice of meat was an especial favorite. He could tap unexpected veins of knowledge in such acquaintances. Robert quickly discovered that the barkeep at a hotel tavern where we used to lunch on the drive back and forth to the farm had an odd assortment of information about American history. The two matched memories over such questions as which president's face appeared on what denomination of bill, and from there went on to assess the presidents themselves.

Other variations in the customary schedule came during the eight weeks of the two Bread Loaf sessions, when Robert gave his annual talks, sometimes formally in the Little Theater but often in front of the fire in the barn behind the Inn, a barn where not so many years before cows had munched their evening hay under the mansard roof. Sunday afternoon baseball games pitting town against gown were regular events at the School. Sitting on the sidelines town wives who the night before had banded together in common hatred of male Saturday night celebrations outstripped each other in support of their errant mates in language that was uninhibited but loyal. The game that outdid all others happened once a year when teachers and members at the Writers' Conference, employees and staff of the Inn, and townsfolk all came to the Homer Noble Farm for a battle royal. The diamond was marked out on our stubbly hayfield, sometimes using one or two of the granite boulders to mark the bases. It was Robert's custom to inspect the field on the morning of the game, and he nearly always decided that one of the rocks, usually the biggest and most obstructive, must be buried to lessen the danger of accident. At noon he would set forth with pick and shovel, outwearing and outlasting fellow workers twenty years or more his juniors. On one occasion he so exhausted himself that his batting performance during the game did not come up to his expectations. He hid his chagrin by disappearing into the woods, to be lured out by a sympathetic teammate. Choosing sides for the players was a touchy business. Robert, as one of the captains, felt imposed upon if he had to accept too many women for his team. And which side was to have the great catcher, Fletcher Pratt, member of the Conference staff, historian, and science fiction writer? Which was to have the swiftest base runner, or a visiting celebrity such as James Farrell, the novelist, or the cricket-playing poet Auden?

Robert's view of softball and of women as ballplayers he summed up succinctly in a piece he contributed to *Sports Illustrated*. He had been invited by this magazine to attend and report on one of the all-star games that interrupt the regular professional baseball seasons. Of softball he said: "If I have shone at all in the all-star games at Bread Loaf in Vermont it has been as a relief pitcher with a softball I despise like a picture window." And of the ladies: "I mustn't count it against them that I envision one in the outfield at a picnic with her arms spread wide open for a fly ball as for a descending man angel." Even in tennis, a quite different game, his attitude toward a female partner in doubles was not markedly dissimilar.

Baseball games were a renewal of boyhood pleasures; in much the same way his decision to farm once more repeated a pattern started almost forty years earlier. His association with cows grew important on the Herbert farm in Franconia about 1915, but they were never his true loves. Although they bore with unorthodox milking hours—at noon and at midnight—they did not take lightly the awkward hands that tried to strip them. Writing to Louis Untermeyer of his difficulties, Robert spoke of "a couple of cows that have to be anchored at both ends as a boat ought to be when you fish for perch or pout," but added some weeks later, "You will be glad to know that my cows and I have composed our differences and I now milk them anchored at one end only." At the Homer Noble Farm he could delegate milking to a hired man, and it occurred at more considerate hours.

Cows were necessary and had to be put up with, but hens were something different. In 1899, when his doctor decreed for him a life in the country to ward off incipient tuberculosis, Robert and Elinor found a half-house outside Methuen, Massachusetts, near the New Hampshire border. Not far away Robert discovered a chicken farm run by a French-Canadian veterinarian, Charlemagne Bricault. The farm specialized in Barred Plymouth Rocks and White Wyandottes "carefully bred from dams of standard weight, whose egg laying record for each succeeding generation was individually known to have increased from year to year. Males are all from two-hundred egg hens." Robert and Dr. Bricault soon formed a loose partnership, and Robert's intermittent but lifelong partiality for hens began. It continued when the quarters in Methuen proved cramped and the Frost family settled on a twenty-acre farm in Derry, New Hampshire. There they remained, on what is now known as a "one-man subsistence farm," until 1909, soon after Robert had joined the faculty of Pinkerton Academy in Derry. As

(1-3)
The annual
baseball game
at the
Homer Noble
Farm.

(Middlebury
College
News Bureau)

(4) In 1956, as
official reporter
for *Sports Illus-
trated,*
R.F. watches
the All-Star
baseball game
in Washington.
"I look at a poem
as a performance.
I look on the poet
as a man
of prowess,
just like an
athlete."

(Susan
Greenburg
Wood, *Sports
Illustrated*)

The Academic Farmer

Prowess on the tennis court.

Lathem and Thompson say in *Robert Frost: Farm-Poultryman*, the last six stanzas of "A Blue Ribbon at Amesbury" contain "lines that serve to heighten any reader's awareness that Robert Frost's years as a farm-poultryman left their indelible mark on his literary career, as a prose writer and as a poet."

It was not until 1940 at Ripton that Robert returned to farming. As I was to continue to do in successive years, I delivered him in late May to the Homer Noble Farm, establishing him there in the main house where there was heat and a telephone, and then returning to Cambridge in preparation for our own family move to Ripton for the summer. I had earlier, at his request, ordered one hundred "unsexed-linked pullorum-free" baby chicks to be delivered to Ripton. The breed was neither White Wyandottes nor Barred Plymouth Rocks but a modern version, Hall's Cross, properly vouched for by a New Hampshire breeder, a former Amherst student and a fellow poet. After a week or so in Cambridge, returning to Vermont to move Robert up to the cabin, I arrived at the farmhouse to discover the kitchen completely taken over by brooders. A powerful smell pervaded the house, and a very happy Robert Frost sat in the living room in front of the large potbellied stove, papers all around him on the linoleum-covered floor, on all available space on the reed organ, while the backless and armless sofa was occupied by government bulletins on the care of poultry. Before long the garage instead of the kitchen became a temporary hen house, and breakfast no longer consisted of cheese sandwiches eaten on the lawn to escape the stench in the house. Within a reasonable time movable hen coops, each like a doghouse with carrying handles fore and aft, were constructed and placed strategically where the hens could fertilize the lawns and surrounding fields. This improvement also had the advantage of relieving Robert of his almost nightly task of lifting to roost one stupid or recalcitrant pullet who did not know how to perch. In a fit of impatience with this backward pupil, Robert once propped her head down for the night in the corner made by two walls.

As May turned into summer in that season of 1940, Robert moved to the cabin according to plan. Our own family—children, cat, kittens, a German refugee who had been a Latin teacher in Hamburg, and a sixteen-year-old Bunty Sage from West Dover—settled into the main house. By then Robert had hired the first of a line of three farmers, Guy Damon, though he proved to be more of a carpenter than a farmer. The organization of the Homer Noble Farm stood at full strength, and the cycle of many succeeding summers there had begun.

My first indiscretion was to rent a mare and a pony, a fulfillment of a childhood wish for a horse—a plea with always the same answer, "Not till the blue snow falls." There were a hundred acres in which to ride and a talented horsewoman, Bunty, who could coach me and initiate the children. Guy Damon had a rattletrap car that got him back and forth between the village and the farm, and we did not immediately need a working team. It was enough that Damon ploughed a vegetable garden for Robert, started clearing fields, cut firewood, and became general manager. By August, though, the mare had reverted to her native lameness and the pony had showed his preference for biting over his willingness to be ridden. They were returned to their owners, and in their stead, for seventy-five dollars, the farm acquired a beautiful black Morgan mare, perfect in every way except that she resolutely refused to back when hitched to a carriage. Ridden or harnessed to a carriage or sleigh, she served both grown-ups and children during the summers or on Christmas holiday visits, and she contributed helpfully to the mobility of Guy Damon.

As early as the preceding season it had become obvious that Robert needed more than writing, walking, teaching, or farming to ease his loneliness. A deserted house on forty acres of land west of the Homer Noble Farm, and only a twenty-minute tramp through the woods, had attracted his attention. It became the lodestone for all his walks. He spent hours planning how to restore it and wondering about its past. He figured costs. He looked for water. We learned after some inquiry that it belonged to a widower who might be persuaded to sell. It could be bought for five hundred dollars and put into shape for a not excessive sum. So Robert acquired the Euber place, as it was called on the old maps, and the work of restoration started. He would use it as a guest house, or if necessary make it an income-producing unit. With Guy Damon, experienced as a carpenter and builder, already on the payroll, hammers began flying by May of 1940 and Robert was again at work as he had been at Concord Corners, showing his architectural skill and his ingenuity. The project itself was of far greater value than the house and a much more effective antidote to grief and loneliness than long sessions with doctors.

Years later Robert was again to show strikingly his uncanny architectural instinct when he designed, almost entirely in his head,

The Academic Farmer

(1)
The farm
at Derry,
New Hampshire.

(Jones Library,
Amherst, Mass.)

(2)
The Euber
Farm in the
winter of 1940
before its
remodeling.

an ell that was added to the Homer Noble farmhouse. The ell included two rooms on split levels and a small shower and toilet unit, and it required the close fitting-in of two short flights of stairs to provide access from the house to the upper and lower rooms of the addition. When the country builder who did the work got into trouble with such problems as joining two pitched roofs at right angles, Robert set him straight with rules of thumb that seemed to derive from his retention of Euclid and school geometry, held firmly and simply in the same mind that retained so much history, poetry, or botany. To this observer, at least, his architectural sense, his ability to come into a room and at once suggest how the furniture could be better arranged, his strong liking for such black-and-white drawings and woodcuts as those of his friend J. J. Lankes, seemed related in some way to his noticeable color blindness. Some readers have even felt in his poetry a quality of black-and-white, of line rather than color. But of course the chief characteristic that underlay his architectural perceptions, as it underlay all his achievements, was his native intellectual power.

By autumn the Euber place was fortified against the winter and ready for active participation in our community life the next summer, when it was to be furnished with pieces from Robert's former home in Amherst and with findings from winter hours spent in antique shops or at the Morgan Memorial salesroom in Boston. It had been promised to Robert's old friends, the George Whichers, who were to occupy it while Professor Whicher taught at the School of English. In late September we all returned to the city, eagerly awaiting another summer and looking forward to the planting of a vegetable garden in a more auspicious situation, cherishing high hopes for greater results from farming and for bigger and more productive hens.

May 1941 brought some changes with the instalment of Ma Jenks as our housekeeper, an Ayreshire cow in the barn, and the beginnings of what was to be a real hen business—two hundred baby chicks. Later in the summer a spotted pony came to keep Curranty, the black mare, company. Ferndale, the cow, had been raised to her splendid and imposing proportions at Bennington by Robert's son, Carol. She claimed a pedigree as long as her horns were wide. Ma Jenks, properly called Mrs. Mary Jenkins, was the daughter of a Scottish schoolmaster brought to New Brunswick by the family of Lord Beaverbrook (as he became), the Canadian and English newspaper magnate. She was the widow of a top guide in the Canadian woods. Until his death her husband and she had managed a hunting lodge privately owned by a New York banker. Ma Jenks became the pivot wheel of our whole operation for the next seventeen summers. Her cooking was unexcelled, and when she "built a salad" all eyes were on the result. Breads, doughnuts, cakes were always present for the children, their friends and visitors. When one of the children came down with a summer cold Ma Jenks, though herself a teetotaler, was not above raiding the family liquor supply to help with her special cough syrup of lemon juice, honey, and bourbon. The brew she made for the haymakers when they came in sweating and plastered with seed was a kind of switchel concocted of barley water, lemon, ginger, and vinegar. She had her prejudices and her political views. Her wisdom guided us all and her acute comments drew us to her bedroom, where the voice of Raymond G. Swing brought us news of World War II through her portable radio, the only one in the house. One of her great joys was to listen to the talk between Robert and his friends as they sat around the dining-room table, her ample proportions filling the doorway to the kitchen, her interruptions firmly pro-British.

The vegetable garden flourished in spite of major mishaps. An unprecedented frost on June 20 nipped back the corn. It grew again, forced under rows of white caps, beautiful white tents that tempted Gillie, the Border collie, to make his own gymkhana, running in and out in an ordered pattern, tossing the covers from alternate hills in gay abandon. The beating Gillie subsequently received and his two-hour banishment to the barn may well have had their roots in Robert's childhood, when he received what seemed equally irrational beatings from his father. At any rate the episode did not permanently dampen Gillie's spirits nor lessen his devotion to his master. Later in the summer, when mouths were watering at the prospect of peas and beet greens, Ferndale escaped from her pasture and lumbered up and down the garden rows, munching and trampling as she went.

The rest of the summer went by much as usual, while Robert was writing, walking, gardening, conferring at Bread Loaf. The days all conspired to present a surface calm, but under the surface emotional storms were often brewing of a temperamental intensity far greater than those physical storms that threatened the barn with their bolts of lightning. Visitors came and went. The schoolhouse bell mounted outside the farmhouse was not always loud enough to warn Robert of unexpected callers; or when he had forgotten that it was time for

The Academic Farmer

"It's one thing to hear the tones in the mind's ear. Another to give them accuracy at the mouth. Still another to implicate them in sentences and fasten them to the page. The second is the actor's gift. The third is the writer's." (From a notebook)

(Alfred Eisenstaedt, Life Magazine © Time Inc.)

supper, the clang of the tongue did not always reach him and bring him down from the woods behind the cabin, where he would be searching for a Canadian holly bush to match one already planted. Persistent reporters in search of copy broke through security and found their victim. Successive years brought different varieties of intrusion. During one season a member of the Writers' Conference walked the mile-and-a-half from Bread Loaf and settled herself under an old apple tree, paperbag lunch in hand, prepared for a long vigil, waiting to tell Robert what "the voices" had bidden her to report. It took more tact than force to return her safely to the Inn, where the resident nurse could persuade her that she might better go home and let her doctor explain that this was not her year to become a writer. Once a good-hearted neighbor, "a loyal friend" as he called himself, suddenly appeared at the cabin armed with a hunting rifle and fortified with the popular combination of beer and Old Duke wine. He had come, he announced, to protect Robert from the communists who in his opinion had so rudely interrupted Robert's informal talk the night before at the local Community House. The vigil lasted for more than an hour, but time and conversation cooled the caller's solicitude if not our own quite legitimate fears.

One of the most dramatic events of our whole Homer Noble experience happened not in summer but in November. We wanted to open the farm for three or four days at Thanksgiving, but Ted's teaching duties at Harvard and our son's attendance at school made for complicated planning. I took Robert on the old Rutland Railroad to stay for one night in the village with our caretakers, the Guy Damons, so that next morning we could open and heat the farmhouse while Ted and our son were driving up from Cambridge, bearing provisions. In the morning, before a sandwich lunch, Robert decided that we should inspect the spring he had dug in the woods beyond the meadow to the west of the house. Going out the door, Robert picked up a box of wastepaper and carried it to the wire incinerator cage behind the garage at the edge of the meadow. In the box he spied an exercise book imposed on its pupils by Shady Hill School, where Ted and I had entered our son. "Never could stand this nonsense," Robert said in effect. "A cow gives ink, water, milk. Check the right answer." He tossed it into the incinerator, and as if in response to his indignation, the fire blazed and to all appearances destroyed the evidences of such unwelcome pedagogy. As we crossed the meadow, about to enter the woods, we looked back and saw flames tearing across the field, spreading through the dry grass. We ran. We telephoned for help. We beat with brooms and smothered with blankets, but uncontrollably the fire tore uphill toward the cabin, surrounded it, and made its way to the great evergreen wilderness to the north—property of the United States Government. The Bread Loaf fire truck arrived and set up at the hand pump in the east pasture where the stock watered. From all directions men carrying water tanks on their backs concentrated on the flames near the buildings. A lumberman and his two sons working in the woods to the north, alerted by the smoke, came on the run to the cabin and seeing the wooden steps about to burst into flames cried out helplessly: "Mrs. Morrison, we need a fire wagon." I answered, "No time! we need to pull the steps away from the building." They did. The cabin was mercifully saved and the fire plunged through the forest, flames crowning the trees with a terrific roar. At dusk when Ted and our son arrived the fire was finally under control, though underground in the duff where decayed needles and leaves lay compacted, the fire smoldered for days. The lumberman cutting timber who had rescued the cabin steps sent a bill amounting to thirty-odd dollars for a wagon and two coats that had actually been beyond the reach of the flames.

From the Forest Service of the United States Department of Agriculture came a bill for $202.42 for "Trespass," carefully designated as not wilful trespass or carelessness, both of which were subject to criminal proceedings. The Department urbanely conceded that it was Robert's "misfortune" rather than "intent."

By 1942 another farm "North of Boston," as the real estate advertisements in the Boston daily papers used to read, became part of Robert's enterprise. On the death of Ira Dow, the Ripton blacksmith and one-time elected representative to the lower house of the legislature at Montpelier, his sixty-acre property came on the market. The Dow place and the Euber, once a single hundred-acre parcel, had been divided over the years. It was only logical to reunite them, to acquire a possible tenant farmer's house complete with barn, blacksmith shop, and sugar house, and also to safeguard the privacy of the Euber farm, whose only access was a right of way through the Dow property. It also pleased Robert, who was sometimes accused of being lazy, to own land that once belonged to the reputedly laziest man in Ripton.

When it grew obvious that the talents and temperament of the Guy Damons were not to be circumscribed by the role of tenant farmer or the kind of tasks Robert expected of them, the Ira Dow place became the home of a new factotum, Robert Dragon. The house was tidied and restored. The barn, with added stalls, sheltered a recently acquired team of work horses, the original cow, now with two heifers, and a new Ayreshire, Fillmore Hamlin, almost as large as Ferndale. The black mare and pony wintered there, spending the summer months at the Homer Noble Farm. The heifers Robert called the "Bennington girls," in allusion to the students of Bennington College, because they knew neither bounds nor limits and roamed all three places leaving devastation behind them.

War restrictions made Robert more conscious of his role as a farmer. To enlarge the hen business, he found a partner in Pinkie Johnson. A mail carrier in the nearby town of Brandon, a local square-dance caller, and a great lover of poultry, Pinkie was a man of parts and versatility. Two hundred chicks were started each summer at the

farm. The cockerels, when ready and when Robert could bring himself to slaughter them, were designated for the dining table at Homer Noble. In October all the birds moved to Pinkie's farm near Brandon. From there he shipped eggs each week to Cambridge. They arrived in tin boxes especially designed by the local plumber. Two fowls a week also made their way to Robert's house in Brewster Street. By the time May came round again the flock was reduced, there were no more eggs, and to Pinkie as part of his reward belonged the remaining birds. The cycle began again late in the month, when boxes of peeping day-old chicks arrived at the Middlebury railroad station addressed to the Homer Noble Farm.

The new tenant farmer posed a wholly different set of problems. Robert Dragon was a master of gay insouciance, of charming unreliability, the full extent of which did not at once appear. With the big team he ploughed the vegetable garden, and during the winter brought in lumber from the woods. He drove us on picnics in a fringed surrey over back roads and once up the steep climb to the modest summit that was later officially named Robert Frost Mountain. He milked the cows—often irregularly—filling two cans for our son and his visiting friends to carry back to us on a daily trek through the woods. The milk was often late in arriving, abandoned on the path while the boys hunted for newts, or left in the hot sun on the Euber terrace while they learned to play chess from the current occupant, Robert's great friend Hyde Cox.

The Academic Farmer

The first chickens at the Homer Noble Farm. (Margaret Johnston)

"Gentlemen: After reading in the June issue regarding Mr. Frost, I have had to wait two months for my 'Yankee ire' to subside, in order to write you regarding this article without 'cuss words' in my letter. We, in Shaftsbury, feel that you have done Mr. Frost a grave injustice by printing this picture of him standing by a hen house, especially in view of the fact that your readers are led to believe that it is his home."

(From a letter to *Yankee* magazine by one of R.F.'s neighbors in South Shaftsbury, August 1938; Dartmouth College Archives)

By now farming included pigs, not the Tamworth bacon variety Robert had dreamed of, but just pigs. They had their ups and downs. An autumn letter to Cambridge from Robert Dragon's wife, Virginia, reported: "We now have little pigs born Saturday, 6 of them. But had Bad luck. one died write after it was Born and In a couple of days the mother step on too and they died. So the other 3 are coming good." Another letter from the same hand announced that the milk separator had broken and that a neighbor was willing to sell his old one for twenty dollars. A check would help "because it is so hard to get butter and the cream is a lot better to churn when separated." The letter went on to elaborate the woes of farming, both for tenant and principal: "Robert [Dragon] has been digging his potatoes. They are half of them rotten. He dug some more of yours. They are most all rotten."

The cows, too, had their share of bad fortune. Ferndale, barren one summer, gored her daughter to death in her attempt to adopt the daughter's bull calf. The bull calf fared no better. His end was ignominious. He was slaughtered, butchered, frozen, and shipped to Cambridge, where I put his tough carcass by hand through an ordinary kitchen meat grinder, providing hamburg to supplement the allotment of meat allowed by war rationing.

As seasons passed, no great changes occurred, but slowly a diminution of the farming enterprise took place, and perhaps a disillusionment. Despite the tensions that entered into any of his relationships, Robert continued to find Bread Loaf a source of friendships and a focus of loyalties. However, relations between Robert as employer and Robert Dragon as tenant farmer became increasingly clouded as Robert received inexplicable grain bills, puzzled at the migratory tendencies of one or another piece of farm equipment, and heard village innuendoes about lumbering operations unaccounted for. Robert decided it might be wise to defer to the wishes of Virginia Dragon and move his tenant farmer family to the Hollow, as the village proper was called, where they could be less isolated and more a part of the community. So, in September 1944 he bought the old Harrington property and gave it to Robert Dragon as a base from which to start a new life. Unfortunately Dragon's new life brought him more than one brush with the law, but the episode shows the good humor and generosity with which Robert Frost could accept an error of judgment, and perhaps also his confidence that he knew how to manage other people's affairs.

Despite this misadventure with one member of the clan, our association with the family continued with the hiring next year of Robert Dragon's older brother, Stafford. With his wife, Ella, and their three children, he moved into the Dow place, and a much more successful era began. Stafford was one of the numerous children of Ed Dragon, a patriarch in the region. Ed's bachelor brother Danny once said that the family name had originally been Icke. Among the progenitors one was known as Icke the Dragoon, and Dragoon, corrupted to Dragon, replaced the rightful name. Whatever their origin, the family had entered Vermont by way of Canada. Ed and Danny were known the country round, more for their charm, their fiddling, dancing, and ballad singing than for their industry. Ed's wife was of different stuff. Irish in ancestry, she bore seventeen children, kept a shining house, served meals on spotless tablecloths, baked and preserved, made her own pharmacopoeia from the local herbs, ruled her children with an iron hand, and in addition to these formidable tasks walked some eight or ten miles five times a week to and from Bread Loaf Inn, where she laundered all the linen. She died at fifty, leaving her children to fend for themselves.

Brains aplenty had the Dragons, but their heritage of industry was unevenly divided. If Stafford's zeal for labor was sometimes reluctant, he was capable of prodigies when he set to. A slight, wiry figure, with fine features in a grained and seamed face, he had eyes as blue as Robert's own. An immaculate dresser in his go-to-meeting clothes, neat and laundered in his working outfit of a T-shirt, trousers, and boots, he knew how to face a camera, and again like Robert, was strikingly photogenic. He could lumber, show horses, carpenter in rough country fashion, build walls — move stones of incredible size into stable position, build a load of hay, and farm. He was a master teamster and with his knowledge of animal husbandry saved many a veterinary bill. He could have gone far if he had been given the education he knew he was capable of; lacking it, he betrayed a deep-seated jealousy of anyone who had been educated. His resentment would come out tiresomely and stubbornly after he had consumed a beer or two. With all his abilities he was diffident about accepting responsibility and making decisions on his own, always afraid he would be found at fault and blamed. A complicated man, with emotional stresses and strains comparable to those of his employer! Although Robert's relations with him often strained his patience, their association survived for seventeen years, greatly to the benefit of each.

With the hiring of Stafford, many changes came to the farm. Stafford brought a team, a cow, and his annual pig. Ella brought her own hens. With the one cow left on the place in addition to his own, Stafford raised calves and soon started his own small cream business. Lost tools and farm machinery were replaced bit by bit. Stafford kept our black mare and pony over the winter, and later the other saddle horses we acquired. Driving Stafford from farm to farm and town to town in search of equipment, I became intimately acquainted with all the outlets for second-hand ploughs, harrows, and hayrakes, and I learned the complicated art of country bargaining. I could soon also name the vulnerable parts of a hay mower, for often at the height of the haying season I was summoned from taking Robert's dictation at the cabin to drive to Middlebury for a replacement for the Pitman rod, the most frequent casualty. Boulders were plentiful, the fields were rough, and the machinery was old. I once came on Stafford in a mood of

"It's knowing what to do with things that counts." (From "At Woodward's Gardens")

(Hanson Carroll)

The Academic Farmer

R.F. with
Shadbush (Chad)
and Gillie.

(Jarvis
Woolverton
Mason)

black despair muttering to himself: "I'm sick of being such a God-damned low-income man with all this friggin' second-hand collateral." But his ingenuities saved the farm, outclassed as it was by the far larger, mechanized farms in the Champlain Valley. His honesty and loyalty made it possible for Robert to live out his days on the Homer Noble place confident that he could do as he wished and accomplish the things most dear to him—his writing above all. With Stafford in charge, Ted and I could leave Robert alone at the farm, assured that he would be watched over and that Stafford's wife Ella would be on call for household chores.

One of Robert's absorbing concerns as a farmer was for water. He did not like it applied cold to his person, but he was always dreaming of an inexhaustible supply that would not give out with every August dry spell, a trial we endured more than once. He had a keen sense for hollows where springs might lie, studying the grasses that grew in them and the slopes leading to them where underground water veins might be waiting to be tapped. He found a spring in the woods beyond the west pasture, had it cleared and walled up with cement, and he obtained permission from the Forest Service to board up and pipe another spring on government land uphill to the east, where gravity could bring it down to the cabin. When both these sources proved insufficient, he hired a professional to drill a driven well, which met all reasonable needs successfully. He also had two ponds bull-dozed into existence and tried to stock them with trout. Although trout did not survive, the ponds made swimming holes and fishing pools where the children could learn to catch calico bass.

In May 1947 Robert made me a present of a mare, named Steeple Bush in honor of Robert's book of poems with that title, which was published at the same time. A year later she had a colt sired by one of the fine Morgan stallions at the United States Morgan Horse Farm in Middlebury. Officially named Shadbush, the colt was called Chad for short. Robert and Stafford rivaled each other in spoiling him, making him the cosset he turned out to be, admirable for a ride but inseparable from his mother till the day of her death.

One project of Robert's turned out disappointingly. This was the planting of a thousand cedar trees in a rough, swampy pasture east of the house. Robert hoped to ensure a supply of durable fence posts, but the deer browsed on the growing tips of the baby cedars and kept them cropped to no more than grass high. Later Robert made a second effort to establish crop trees. The occasion for this renewed attempt was an irreparable loss Ted and I suffered. Robert had been close to our son Bobby ever since his boyhood. In 1954 the boy had become a young man in his twenties. Driving to a ski slope over a snowy Vermont road, he was killed by a passing car while trying to remove a broken tire chain. Partly as a memorial to him, Robert hopefully supervised the setting out, in a neglected hayfield high up in the woods, of a thousand seedling balsams and a thousand Norway spruce. Again the deer profited, cropping the balsams as fast as they put out growing tips. The spruces took hold, but Homer Noble manpower was never enough to keep down the fast-growing soft maples that threatened to choke the spruces as they grew.

The major hayfields around the house were eventually cleared of boulders, leaving the fields surrounded by a formidable glacial barricade. At least Robert could no longer say

> I farm a pasture where the boulders lie
> As touching as a basket full of eggs.

But he could and did boast of the fine crops of hay cut from the now clean meadows. The vegetable garden flourished despite its annual battle against deer, woodchucks, and premature frost. An apple orchard rose along its northern edge, planted with young McIntoshes waiting to be grafted with scions from old varieties: Sweet Bough, Cole's Quince, Lowland Raspberry, and Porter. Alas, neither Robert nor Stafford lived to see the grafting accomplished.

We carried on with the horses, breaking and training Chad until he and Steeple made an imposing pair at local horse shows. Robert shared in the pride Ted and I took in our daughter's horsemanship. She added two horses of her own to the roster, a gray mare and a gelding from the Morgan Horse Farm who under her skilled hands overcame his fear of men and turned into a prize winner easily

The Academic Farmer

The
last haying
at the
Homer Noble
Farm.
(Anne Morrison
Smyth)

managed by man or woman. And later it took many weeks and great diplomacy on her part to persuade Robert that it would not be wise to add to the overcrowded stable at Homer Noble a government-owned mare she had trained to saddle and who won the coveted honor of best Pleasure Horse in the annual 100 Mile Ride held each year at Woodstock, Vermont.

Much earlier in his life, speaking of his years at Derry, Robert had written to Louis Untermeyer: "It is not fair to farmers to make me out a very good or laborious farmer. I have known hard times but no special shovel-slavery." To another correspondent he wrote in 1915: "I kept farm, so to speak, for nearly ten years, but less as a farmer than as a fugitive from a world that seemed to 'disallow me'." After the death of Elinor, his desperate need for a sustaining way of life, in combination with the circumstances of the war years, made of the Homer Noble project both a revival of his farming predilections and an application of them to a new purpose. But gradually it became clear that farming with any hope of profit was no longer possible on a rough, small-scale tract well up in the hills. Perhaps it might work with three stalwart sons willing to join in a family enterprise, but not with hired help. Our experiment with maple sugaring finally made the point very obvious. We sugared for two or three years, hiring a man to help Stafford. It was an exhilarating sight to watch the white steam rising from the sugar house, the horse-drawn sap tank, the buckets hanging on trees, the great pile of cordwood ready to stoke the fire hour after hour to keep the evaporator at its even heat. But in the final accounting, without any allowance for the cost of custom-designed labels or for the hours spent in marketing the tins of syrup, we still barely broke even. Nothing was laid aside to replace equipment, nor was there any profit to help install modern methods using pipes and plastic sap buckets. Indeed to modernize would only have reduced what had been a gay and picturesque operation to dull profit-making efficiency.

Though farming for other than table vegetables and apples, and hay for the horses, eventually petered out, the Homer Noble place continued to play an indispensable part in Robert's life. My husband, called on to speak after Robert's death at a memorial meeting in the Ripton Community House, reminded his audience: "Ripton was a place of refuge and restoration to him, where he could renew acquaintance with the 'country things' he speaks of in one of his poems, things he never ceased to love and need, though he was a citizen of the world and came to be as much at home in cities and capitals as he was botanizing in the woods and meadows." It was from the Homer Noble Farm in Ripton that in 1954 Robert went to Brazil, accompanied by his daughter Lesley, on a mission for the State Department. To the farm he returned from England in 1957, with honors from the Universities of Oxford, Cambridge, and Dublin, and from the farm he went in 1962 to Russia and his meeting with Khrushchev. The farm was the setting for the documentary film made by the USIA in 1960, and in 1962 most of the Holt, Rinehart and Winston film, "A Lover's Quarrel," was photographed there. The major part of his later writing occurred as he sat in the Morris chair at the cabin with his homemade lapboard propped on his knee in front of him. In fact it would be safe to say that the greater part of his poetry started in that chair, which he had bought while he was a student at Harvard in 1897 and which he carried with him to Derry and later to Franconia, Ann Arbor, and Amherst and to its final destination, the Homer Noble Farm.

(From the George Brown-Plymouth State College Collection)

R.F. at Plymouth in his Morris chair. "There is danger of forgetting that poetry must include the mind, as well as the emotions . . . The mind is dangerous and must be left in . . . The poet can use the mind in fear and trembling. But he must use it." (An interview in *The Scotsman*, Edinburgh, May 1957, speaking about young poets.)

47

III

Barding Around

"I'm terrible about my lectures. In my anxiety to keep them as long as possible from becoming part of my literary life, I leave them rolling round in my head like clouds rolling round in the sky . . . Their chief value to me is for what I pick up from them when I cut across them with a poem under emotion."

—Letter to R. P. T. Coffin.

In 1906, six years after settling on the Magoon place in Derry, New Hampshire, Robert began to realize the ultimate futility of his life as a "hen-man." Impelled by several motives and decisive as always, he set about planning a different course. He was half aware that without the backing of his friend, Dr. Bricault, who was about to return to his practice as a veterinarian, he would not prosper in the poultry business. He was even more conscious of his growing need of a larger income for himself and his family. He was also enraged by what he considered the attitudes of his fellow townsmen toward his casual farming and vexed by the modesty of the annuity he received under his grandfather's will. Time and time again he spoke to me of the teller in the Derry bank who, when Robert deposited his quarterly check, had said, "Some more of your hard-earned money." In fact the scar left by this episode lasted with Robert till the end of his life. He hated banks. He welcomed it as a major relief to have me cash his checks, thus sparing him the agony of watching the teller verify his signature. When he did go into the Harvard Trust in Cambridge, he was not the same Robert whom one met on the street. No longer confident, he somehow took on the posture of a simple country man about to deposit a small check, worried lest it not be good. Once in Vermont Ted and I, viewing the wreckage of a smashed buggy brought home by our daughter, Anne, after her pony had bolted, were joined by Robert. He met Anne with a sympathy that went back to an accident of his own at the railroad station in Derry. His little black mare, Eunice, shied at the approach of the train, upsetting and damaging his new red sleigh. What really bothered him most was what he imagined to be the secret delight of the onlookers.

After abandoning the poultry business, Robert thought of a return to teaching, and began looking for a suitable post. In his first attempt he was rebuffed by the chairman of the Derry school board, who would not even open the dossier Robert offered in support of his qualifications. Then, partly through the warm recommendation of the Reverend William Wolcott, whom he had met in Lawrence, Massachusetts, and who had tried to befriend him with well-meant if not well-judged counsel about his poems, he secured a more desirable position at Pinkerton Academy. From this base in education he gradually entered on the life of what he called "barding around."

Those who heard Robert in his later years may find it hard to believe the struggles that his early public appearances cost him. Invited in 1906 to read from his poems before the Men's League of a Congregational Church in Derry, he found himself utterly without the requisite nerve. The pastor, the Reverend Charles Merriam, stood in for him and read "The Tuft of Flowers." Robert first overcame his initial trepidation in 1909 when he gave a talk to a convention of New Hampshire teachers held in the Robinson Female Seminary at Exeter. Not that this small triumph came easily! He often told me of his terror as he looked over the room in which he was to speak, terror so great that he went outdoors and filled his shoes with pebbles, a cutting diversion against the ordeal he was about to face. Not satisfied with this distraction, he doused the back of his neck with water from the yard pump, temporarily conquering his lifelong fear of the effect of cold water on his system. Such were the first ventures of a man who could later hold spellbound audiences of thousands. Yet all the while his sensitivity persisted. Even in his last years he could retreat to the cabin at the Homer Noble Farm in deep depression at some fancied slight after one of his appearances, perhaps only because a child of whom he was fond had failed to praise the talk he had just given at Bread Loaf.

Delivery of the Phi Beta Kappa poem at Tufts College in June 1915 marked the first of a long series of lecture-readings which ended only with his final hospitalization. His face became familiar to travelers on trains, to porters and dining car stewards, and later to passengers on the airways. Necessity ruled the choice of his first engagements: he took what came his way. But as Robert's inborn sense of the dramatic increased and enabled him to draw his audiences to him freely and confidently, he began to be pressed by invitations from all quarters. As the years went on, his lectures and readings fell into two main groups: Amherst, Michigan, Yale, Harvard, and Dartmouth claimed him for the longer regular appointments; more than a hundred other institutions claimed him for short stays annually or occasionally.

It was at Amherst that the pattern of Robert's relation to academic life emerged. It was a pattern made up of two elements: his equivocal attitude toward education and the friends he made in spite of this attitude. As Robert put it in his own words: "I'm imperfectly academic and no amount of association with the academic will make me perfect. It's too bad for I like the academic in my way, and up to a certain point the academic likes me." At Amherst, where he had been brought by President Alexander Meiklejohn in 1917 in the hope of putting new life into the English Department and of shaking students and faculty out of what Meiklejohn considered their complacency, Robert could love education—his own kind—and hate the professors while finding lifelong friends among them. He could advise students, following his own principle of "freedom in departure," to escape from college and return only after shedding educational patter and developing some ideas of their own. He confirmed his belief in what he called "education by presence" through seminars held by four undergraduates in a room at Beta Theta Pi House. Long sessions before his own hearth fire brought together students such as Gardner Jackson, Charles Foster, and George Yeh, men who many years later in Washington and Minnesota carried on with him discussions begun in Amherst days. With Gardner Jackson the theme was Justice against Injustice, a major preoccupation of Robert's thought and poetry. The case of Sacco and Vanzetti entered into their give and take. In 1961, at the home of Charles Foster, who had become a professor at the University of Minnesota, talks about the place of metaphor and the writings of Emerson

"Justice! and the next word you think of is mercy. What holds the two together— what holds any pair? Action. Life is a mechanic mixture in which matter and spirit are made one by the paddle of action."

(Alfred Eisenstaedt, Life Magazine © Time Inc.)

carried on explorations begun long since in the thirties. It was to the Embassy of Nationalist China that Robert, during his years as Consultant in Poetry to the Library of Congress, went for luncheons and political talk with Ambassador George Yeh. Beyond the academic circle at Amherst, Robert found an audience of the kind he frequently described as the best he could ask for—the people of a small college town.

He encountered one charge at Amherst that he could not take lightly. He did not relish being dubbed "anti-intellectual." If an intellectual is a man who incessantly applies his mind, day and night, to questions ranging from the metaphysical to the design of an ell for a house, from the poems of Horace and Catullus to the fears, hopes, and health of his own life and of his family and friends, then few men have equaled Robert as an intellectual. The poet who could say, "I'm lost in admiration for science—its plunge of the mind, the spirit into the material universe," can hardly be taxed with hostility to the mind and its uses. To quote from his own words in "Departmental," a poem that pokes sly fun at academic departmentalism by way of the behavior of ants, Robert was

> one
> Of the hive's inquiry squad
> Whose work is to find out God
> And the nature of time and space, . . .

The charge of anti-intellectualism must have arisen from his innate conservatism, partly the conservatism of a country man and a halfway farmer, partly rooted in a more general skepticism toward facile hopes of social progress. His attitude toward the New Deal was, for example, equivocal to say the least. Earth was the right place for love, he said in "Birches," but was not likely to become an easier place in which to save one's soul or one's integrity, as he put it elsewhere. One age is not likely to be better or worse than another—the burden of dispute in "The Lesson for Today." Perhaps what has exasperated some recognized intellectuals in Robert's work is the absence from it of any generous vision of a world redeemed and made perfect by any kind of political program or alignment. Generous he could be and often was in his personal life, but this particular kind of generous poetic vision was not his to give. "Trial by Existence" was his theme, and well chosen as the title of Elizabeth Sergeant's sympathetic biography.

Robert's return to Amherst in 1949 after the temporary break that followed Elinor's death was more than a reconciliation: it was a homecoming. Relieved by President King's successor, Charles Cole, of the pressures that came with fixed residence, Robert visited the college twice a year, spending two weeks in spring and fall at the Lord Jeffrey Inn. There, with his faithful Gillie, he occupied two rooms at the end of a corridor, with windows overlooking the garden and access to a back door for unnoticed exits and entrances. Under the watchful eye of his former student, Professor Armour Craig, he visited classes, spent evenings at fraternity houses, and dined with faculty friends, carrying on talk begun many years earlier. He was a welcome guest in the homes of friends of long standing: the Otto Manthey-Zorns, the Ted Bairds, the Newton McKeons, the George Whichers, the Roy Elliots, and the Reuben Browers. He renewed old friendships in the town, such as that with Warren R. Brown, the real estate dealer who had found the Frost family their first rented house. He hobnobbed with the president of one of the Amherst banks. He was in and out of the Robert Frost room at the Jones Memorial Library, where his friend Charles R. Green presided over that notable collection of Frostiana. It was here that an amusing incident occurred. Robert was looking, with Mr. Green, for a missing manuscript. Forgetting what it might contain, Green opened a chest only to find lying in plain view a packet of letters. Quickly lowering the lid, he said, "Those don't belong to the library. They are Larry Thompson's." To which Robert replied, "Nothing is secret from me," and picked up the packet, which proved to consist of four of his own letters, written in 1886 when he was twelve years old, to Sabra Peabody, his childhood sweetheart. One of them reads:

> There are not many girls I like but when I like them I fall dead in love with them and there are not many I like just because I can have some fun with them like I can Lida but I like you because I can't help myself and when I get mad at you I feel mad at myself to.
>
> From your loveing   *Rob*

Robert forgave Lawrance Thompson for not having told him that the letters had been discovered, and Thompson printed them in his *Selected Letters of Robert Frost.*

Freed from formal academic obligations, Robert could luxuriate in the warm friendship and generous hospitality of President Charles Cole and his wife Kitty. To be greeted at the door by the Coles' major-domo eased Robert's travel weariness when he arrived for Parents' Day, for a meeting of the Board of Trustees, or for his annual reading in Johnson Chapel. After the retirement of President Cole, his successor, Calvin Plimpton and his wife Ruth carried on the tradition of adopting Robert. It was their fate to endure the legion of cameramen who invaded their house for an evening during the filming of the documentary, *A Lover's Quarrel.* After Robert's death, it was President Plimpton who presided both at the memorial service in Johnson Chapel and at the dedication ceremonies for the Robert Frost Library at Amherst College, ceremonies during which President John F. Kennedy and Archibald MacLeish made memorable addresses on Robert and his work.

The three years Robert spent at the University of Michigan were interspersed among the many more years he devoted to Amherst. He

Barding Around

"The only certain freedom's in departure." (From *"How Hard It Is to Keep from Being King When It's in You and in the Situation"*)

(From *"A Lover's Quarrel with the World"*)

later described his association with Michigan as marked by "sickness and scatteration." Somehow the family never accepted Ann Arbor as home, though the senior Frosts might have made the adjustment if the problems of their children had not intervened. Academically and publicly his first Michigan year as Poet in Residence in 1921 proved a notable success. Town and gown received him enthusiastically, posing what President Marion L. Burton jocularly called a threat to the popularity of football. He helped the editors of the college literary magazine, *Whimsies,* to arrange a series of poetry readings, and persuaded Amy Lowell, Carl Sandburg, Padraic Colum, Witter Bynner, and Louis Untermeyer to participate. But with the family all was not well. Lesley, Irma, and Carol, unable to accept the life at Ann Arbor, left for Vermont before the end of the year to join Marjorie, who had remained in school at North Bennington. Elinor and Robert stayed through commencement, when he received an honorary A.M. with a generous citation which did not console him for the lost hours he might have spent on his own writing.

Uncertain of reappointment, Robert signed up during the summer for winter readings in places as widely separated as Vermont, Texas, and Louisiana. In early October he received a telegram from President Burton offering him the title of Fellow in the Creative Arts, adding as a climactic inducement that the donor was prepared to make the endowment permanent. The year started under a cloud. Elinor, after settling all four children in the East, moved to Ann Arbor where some weeks later she was joined by her husband, exhausted by travel and talks and suffering from another of his bouts with influenza—one of the five he was to endure in the weeks following. Away for Christmas and again for a spring vacation prolonged by sickness—his own and that of the children—he became aware that perhaps his absences were to blame for smaller audiences than he had faced in the previous year. Although the students openly voiced their hope that his days at Michigan would last to the end of his life, Robert wrote to his friend Sidney Cox that he didn't "know what I think of the berth now I'm about to rub my eyes and climb out of it. The sleeping in it was only so so." In June 1923 he resigned, prepared to return to Vermont and devote himself to his poetry.

Despite the rupture, he had not cut his ties with Michigan as finally as he supposed. President Burton, before his death in February 1925, persuaded Robert to return to Ann Arbor, inviting him to spend the rest of his days there with a minimum of obligations but with some scheduled meetings. The prospect of turning from what he called "part-time teacher" into "no-time teacher" with the "detached attachment" he had longed for seemed near at hand, but was never to be realized. In the autumn of 1925 he began his last Michigan stay as Fellow in Letters, but he did not find communication easy with the new president, Clarence Little. Robert and President Burton were of one accord about philosophy, poetry, and education, but with President Little, later famous for his Institute of Cancer Research at Bar Harbor in Maine, Robert always felt the conflict of opposites that marked so much of his thinking and talking. Often equivocal in his attitudes, Robert was also equivocal in his views of science. Within his layman's limitations he understood Niels Bohr, Albert Einstein, and Jacques Loeb and was fascinated by them, but he was repelled by the rigidity of thought he found in scientists of less achievement. One of the books always by his bedside was Darwin's account of his voyage on the *Beagle,* a book given him by Clarence Little himself as a result of a dinner conversation. But what he called the "cocksuredness" of professional scientists upset him deeply. He found more of this "cocksuredness" at Michigan than he had at Amherst, and it contributed to his malaise at Ann Arbor.

The year 1925 nonetheless brought him many lasting friendships. Dean Joseph Bursley took the Frosts into his own home while they awaited the arrival of their furniture. The editorial board of the literary magazine, now called *The Inlander,* included three students who became friends for life: Sue Grundy Bonner, Mary Elizabeth Cooley, and Dorothy Tyler. "The Three Graces," as he called them, have continued, each in her own way, to preserve a true image of Robert in the memories of old and young. A friend of a different sort he found in Wade Van Dore, who turned up one day at the Frost house on Pontiac Street. Not a registered student but a wanderer, a disciple of Thoreau, and an amateur poet, he had written Robert in 1922, admiring Robert's own poems and at the same time asking where he could find a place in which to work only to keep himself clothed and sheltered in a life devoted to poetry. Delighted as always by such a display of independence in a man with concerns so close to his own, Robert recommended him to Willis Herbert, a farmer neighbor in Franconia, New Hampshire. Van Dore spent the following winter in Franconia, camping out in a home-built shack on land belonging to Herbert. Next summer Robert and Van Dore met and walked the mountains, botanizing as they went.

A letter written in May 1926 to his friend John Bartlett and published in *Robert Frost and John Bartlett* by Bartlett's daughter, Margaret B. Anderson, gives both a background for his final break with Michigan and a picture of the conflicting emotions, the pressures, and the insecurities of his "barding around":

> We're going east again said the pendulum. This was no go this year, or rather it was too much go and what wasn't go was come. Marjorie's long illness . . . kept Elinor with her in Pittsfield Mass and me commuting for months. Every week or so I would run the water out of the pipes and leave the house here to freeze. It wasn't exactly in the contract to try to keep it up here with the children back there and such things likely to happen again. And any way I want a farm . . . Amherst, Dartmouth, Bowdoin and Connecticut Wesleyan are going to give me a living next year for a couple of weeks in each of them. The rest of the time I shall be clear away from the academic, feeding pigeons hens dogs or anything you advise for the pleasure or profit in it . . . I ran away from two colleges in succession once and they took revenge by flattering me back to teach in college. Now I am running away again and it looks as if they would come after me. I'll probably end with one of the ponderous things in bed with me on my chest like an incubus.

R.F. in his Brewster Street study.

(Edward Fitzgerald, UPI, Boston)

The colleges from which Robert ran away in succession while he was a student were, of course, Dartmouth and Harvard. Both did in fact lure him back to teach in one or another capacity. His official positions at Harvard began as early as 1925, when he was elected a member of the Overseers' Committee to Visit the English Department, although I never heard him speak of actually carrying out a visitation or attending the annual committee dinner. In the year after his great public success with the Norton Lectures, Harvard conferred on him the degree of Litt.D. In the following year he became a member of the Board of Overseers itself, one of the two supreme governing boards in the university hierarchy, and he was appointed chairman of its committee to visit the Arnold Arboretum. Despite his tastes for botanizing, this was an office to which he gave more thought than presence. During the autumn of 1939, President James Bryant Conant named him Ralph Waldo Emerson Fellow in Poetry, a post he held for two years. As a condition of accepting it, he was compelled to resign from the Board of Overseers. In 1941 he became Fellow in American Civilization and an

58

Associate of Adams House, one of the residential and educational subunits into which the undergraduate college is divided. As a salaried member of the Harvard community he met with students in the various houses, speaking before special groups; and at Adams House, under the mastership of David Mason Little, he conducted a weekly seminar in writing. "Please don't call this a course in creative writing," he once said of it. "I hate that word. Writing's writing and that is all there is to it."

During the months following Pearl Harbor, Harvard, like other colleges, took on the appearance of a military training camp. The overwhelming majority of undergraduates were in uniform, special programs at the Business School and elsewhere were organized for officers and officer candidates, many of whom brought their wives and children to Cambridge, while blue-skirted Waves marched in phalanx from the Radcliffe dormitories toward the Yard. Robert was again appointed to a special post, this time called Honorary Ralph Waldo Emerson Fellow in Poetry. Part of the object of this post was to enable trainees and their families to share in the intellectual and artistic resources of the community. Robert gave many talks, some open to the public, some to designated groups. He appeared at the Medical School, and at the Tavern Club and the St. Botolph Club in Boston. He spent long evenings with Dr. Merrill Moore, a younger member of the Fugitive group of poets. Merrill would often take Robert to dinner in Chinatown or at the Rib Room in the Somerset Hotel. Dinner would be followed by a visit to one of Merrill's psychiatric patients, Merrill driving while Robert listened to him recite his own sonnets and worried about the degree of attention Merrill was giving to the road.

In the course of these years Robert came especially to value his association with certain students who told him of their war experiences, particularly one who had survived campaigns in the Pacific as a carrier pilot. All his life Robert paid tribute to bravery, and often concerned himself, not without misgivings, with wondering how he would have behaved in war as opposed to the very different battles he was called on to fight with himself or with circumstance. "Courage is the virtue that counts most," he often said. In *A Masque of Mercy*, putting the point another way, he gives to his character Jesse Bel the lines that she speaks to Jonah:

> Your courage failed. The saddest thing in life
> Is that the best thing in it should be courage.

A special Harvard group with whom Robert enjoyed frequent exchanges consisted of the Nieman Fellows, practicing journalists competitively chosen each year from all parts of the country and brought to the university to study or explore any of its offerings or resources they might choose. One of the Fellows Robert met was William Pinkerton, now an administrative officer of the university, who summed up in a letter Robert's effect on the Niemans of his year:

> I'm sure you are not aware of the magnitude of your personal victory in winning the love and admiration of every one of the Nieman Fellows — split as we were among guilders and non-guilders, leftists and rightists, interventionists and isolationists, reds and Tories. But we are agreed at the end of the year that you had given us our most fruitful and pleasant sessions.

Robert's adroitness in dealing with the press and its representatives is illustrated at length in Edward Connery Lathem's *Interviews with Robert Frost.*

Robert's experience at Harvard was both like and unlike his experience at other colleges. His public success was as conspicuous as ever, he made and kept friends as always, but he was not altogether free from the tensions he had felt elsewhere. His equivocal attitude toward the academic persisted, and personal relations from time to time resulted in those clashes of opposites he had known on other campuses. Moreover, a part of him stood in awe of Harvard. On at least one occasion this awe seemed to revive momentarily the terror he felt in his earliest ventures in facing a public. The man who introduced him to the usual packed audience told me that Robert's face, while he waited to go to the lectern, had lost its color and turned sickly, and his hands were trembling. He looked hardly capable of carrying through with his reading. But as a sentence or two brought a ripple of amusement from his audience, his color came back, his hands grew firm, and he was off and away with one of his brilliantly engaging performances.

When his formal Harvard appointments came to an end, Robert continued, of course, to give single talks and readings at the university. Among the later ones, I particularly recall an occasion when his audience was embarrassingly, almost riotously, large. My daughter Anne and her husband had delivered him to the hall by car and naturally expected to be admitted. An overflow crowd was to be accommodated by a broadcast to an adjoining room, but the corridors leading to the lecture hall were packed with resentful people who could not get into either room. Anne had to be forcibly propelled through the wedged bodies by a formidable policeman, and a disappointed woman kicked at her as they went by. Such were some of the unanticipated effects of barding around.

By the spring of 1943 Robert began to realize that successful as his life at Harvard had proved, the university could not offer him a permanent and adequately rewarding position. An interview took place with President Conant during which Mr. Conant offered him the curatorship of the Poetry Room in the Lamont Library at a yearly stipend considerably less than the fees he was then receiving for single lectures. The interview was not a happy one. Not long after, by a fortunate coincidence, Professor Ray Nash called on him from Hanover,

instructed by President Ernest Martin Hopkins to discover whether Robert might be persuaded to join the faculty at Dartmouth College. President Hopkins realized, according to Mr. Nash, that "the small world of Hanover was fast becoming transformed into a Navy outpost" and that Robert was needed as never before. On the first of July, Robert was appointed George Ticknor Fellow in the Humanities, a post he was to hold until his permanent return to Amherst in 1949.

President Hopkins asked for "no cut and dried responsibilities or obligations but that beginning in the fall, you should contribute the major part of your time to the College for counsel and advice to students, for association with faculty members, and for occasional talks or lectures here and there within the college community." Robert spent six happy years at Hanover, using the Hanover Inn as his headquarters and enjoying the hospitality and friendship of his colleagues. On Thursdays, from October to January, I would put him on the train to Hanover for a stay that would last until Sunday night. I could be reasonably sure that all would go well and that no crisis would occur.

Once I had trouble. While driving him to the train, I made the unforgivable mistake of failing to take Robert's side in an account he gave of a dinner-party argument the night before. Perhaps overconfident in my past successes in persuading Robert that many of his so-called enemies were really friends, I tried again, but to no avail. My timing may have been unfortunate; perhaps he was already coming down with a cold. At Lebanon he was met by Professor Nash, who found him ready to disagree with any proposal. The next day he had one of his severe colds, and three or four days later he was taken to the hospital with pneumonia. Many weeks passed before I was forgiven for causing it!

In February 1949 Robert wrote to John Sloan Dickey, successor to President Hopkins, a letter which he said gave him "a good deal of pain." In it he told President Dickey that he was being asked to return to Amherst, "to the college of my first and longest employment and on terms so extravagantly generous that I couldn't expect anyone else to match them." He went on to say: "But I must beg you to let me leave you now with your blessing. Please understand that what takes me away is not just more money, though that has to be considered even with the improvident. It is largely the appeal of being provided for at one stroke for the rest of my time in and out of education."

Besides his major engagements at Amherst, Michigan, Harvard, Yale, and Dartmouth, Robert's barding around took him to innumerable high schools, boarding schools, colleges, universities, clubs, forums, and institutes of every imaginable kind. Some of them he visited frequently or even annually, others for single performances. His early lecture-readings back in the thirties naturally began on a modest scale. For several years Elinor kept track of his commitments in a five-cent school copybook. She noted dates, addresses, and fees — a hundred dollars here, two hundred there. Sometimes Robert himself put down his engagements and also jotted headings and themes he meant to talk about. A particularly interesting notebook leaf in his hand records a series of such themes. One of them, "Sympathy with Presidents," suggests the fascination that power had for him. Over the word "Presidents" is scrawled on a slant an even more characteristic topic, "Making Form." Another entry reads: "Weakness that would Try to Repeat Successes in Wit Humor or—I pray to be forgiven if I have twice or thrice traded on my success with not so much as a locution even." (An omission seems to have occurred here, perhaps "change of locution.") Still another topic, with a star beside it for emphasis, is the question "Can Poetry be Taught?"

To list anything like the total number of appearances Robert made in all parts of the country, from major cities to local communities, would obviously not be feasible—despite the injustice of omissions, both to the institutions concerned and to the many friends his visits brought him. A handful of examples must be allowed to stand for the hundreds of engagements recorded in the calendars I kept for him during his last twenty-odd years.

The South was well-ploughed territory in Robert's reading and lecturing tours. His earliest regular commitment there was to his friend Professor Clifford Lyons, who was teaching at the University of Florida in Gainesville. When Elinor died, it was Clifford Lyons who accompanied Lesley to Jacksonville for the cremation. Until 1962 Robert continued his annual visits with Lyons, transferring them to the University of North Carolina at Chapel Hill when his friend joined the faculty of that institution. Among the places to which Robert returned repeatedly, where he was welcomed as if coming home, were Agnes Scott College at Decatur, Georgia, and the University of Georgia at Athens. Robert would make his annual stay at both places toward the end of January. At Agnes Scott a borrowed overcoat, more suitable to the southern climate than his heavy traveling coat, would be waiting for him each year. He relished the fine talk and hospitality extended by his special friend, Dr. Wallace Alston, the president of the college, and by Miss Emma Laney, the head of the English Department. At Athens his special pleasure lay in his friendship with Dr. Hugh Hodgson, chairman of the Department of Music, an organist and pianist whose playing, accompanied by ebullient comments, pleased Robert as much as it expanded his knowledge of music. One of Robert's amateur interests was archaeology, and at Athens he found in Dr. Clemens De Baillou and his wife, Katharine, congenial fellow diggers. I still have an Indian arrowhead—pre-Columbian, Robert told me—that the three of them found on one of their exploratory walks.

In 1931, Robert wrote to his friend, Frederick G. Melcher, editor of the *Publishers' Weekly:* "I am going to ask you very privately for a piece of advice. Do you think I would derogate from my dignity or aloofness or anything if I did a series of lectures (so to call them) on poetry this winter at the New School for Social Research. I'm not afraid of the

(1)
A page
from an early
engagement
book.

(Courtesy
of Alfred C.
Edwards)

(2)
"I am a great
equalitarian:
I try to spend
most of my time
with my
equals."

Barding Around

"Don't tell the poem in other and worse English of your own to show you understand it.
But say something of your own based on the poem (not an opinion of it though!)."

(Dartmouth College Archives)

radicals . . ." Apparently Fred Melcher's answer encouraged him to accept Alvin Johnson's invitation, especially as Robert felt that this New York series would give him an audience different from those he faced from the usual academic platform. The six lectures he delivered at that time were the precursors of many later talks and the start of a lasting friendship with Alvin Johnson.

At Kenyon College in Gambier, Ohio, Robert was for twenty-odd years almost a member of the family of President Gordon Chalmers and his wife, Roberta, herself a poet. He shared with them not only pleasure in their children, but participation in the academic community. In Kenyon, he found a center of the kind of intellectual talk he was eager for. Philosophy, poetry, mathematics — he pursued them all. He went to baseball games with his friend John Crowe Ransom, who had been the guiding genius of the Fugitive group of poets. The climactic event in his Kenyon association came in October 1959, when a three-day conference was held in his honor. The elaborate program brought distinguished men from all disciplines — Thomas Reed Powell from the Harvard Law School, Kenneth B. Murdock from the Harvard English Department, L. A. G. Strong and Walter Havighurst, novelists, Marston Morse from the Institute for Advanced Study, and the Right Reverend Henry Hobson, Bishop of Southern Ohio. Robert himself gave an address and reading, and the Dramatic Club of the college staged a performance of *A Masque of Mercy*.

Late in 1946 a group of students at the Massachusetts Institute of Technology asked President James Killian if Robert could be persuaded to visit the Institute and give a reading. The students, according to Dean Theodore Wood, "wanted a first hand look at a practising humanist." With the permission of Dartmouth, Robert agreed to a four-week session starting in November 1947, with the understanding that he would come "a-visiting for one main lecture and some lesser group meetings." He added: "your flattering call on me for a little help has set me thinking on many things about schools as they are, ought to be, and may be about to become. Humanities is a good name to trade under. We both trade under it, I notice." From the time of Robert's visit, the humanities have become more and more important in the curriculum of the Institute.

All during the years when Robert was strenuously lecturing, traveling, and teaching, he confronted family problems and crises which were inevitably interrelated with his far-flung visitations. He and Elinor could live where his appointments demanded, but to provide for the children posed other difficulties. In 1934 the first of a series of blows occurred. Marjorie, their second daughter, after her recovery from tuberculosis, had married Willard Fraser and was living in Billings, Montana, when her first child, Elinor Robin, was born. Septicemia immediately set in. After six terrible weeks in the Billings hospital she was flown to the Mayo Clinic in Minnesota in the hope that what Robert referred to as "the miracles of modern science" might avert the threatened tragedy. But the hope was not rewarded. After enduring a temperature of 110 degrees, the highest ever recorded at the Clinic, she died. In a letter to Louis Untermeyer (surely one of the most moving letters ever written), Robert said: "But curse all doctors who for a moment let down and neglect in childbirth the scientific precautions they have been taught in school. We thought to move heaven and earth—heaven with prayers and earth with money. We moved nothing. And here we are Cadmus and Harmonia not yet placed safely in changed forms." Robert was alluding to a lyric interlude in Matthew Arnold's "Empedocles on Etna," describing the familiar legend according to which Cadmus and Harmonia were metamorphosed into "two bright and aged snakes" . . . "placed safely in changed forms"—after disasters had destroyed their children. Louis Untermeyer quotes Robert as calling Arnold's lines "My favorite poem long before I knew what it was going to mean to us," and Louis speaks of Marjorie as "the Frosts' dearest jewel." Her loss was Robert's great tragedy and a final blow to Elinor.

The death of Marjorie was one of those brute accidents that can befall any parents; but the case of Robert's only son, Carol, was another matter. Carol had had his difficulties since childhood. He did not fit easily into any usual pattern. He wrote poems, but he was not a reader. He was a perfectionist in what he undertook; he would work himself to exhaustion in his garden. When Robert once took him to task for his meticulous weeding, Carol said to him in effect, "But you try to make your poems perfect, don't you?" It was hard for Robert to explain that farming was usually accompanied by a profit motive when it was Carol's firm belief that complete dedication, whether to farming or to poetry, should be its own reward, without any thought of financial gain. Remarks by his neighbors that happened by coincidence to resemble what he himself had said made Carol suspect that he was being watched. Robert tried many expedients in an attempt to settle him in a way of life in which his sensitiveness, his love of children, and his talent with animals and horticulture could be at home. These ranged from sheep raising in California to growing tung nuts in Florida. In an effort to help Carol become more of a member of the community in which he lived, Robert bought him a pew in the church at Bennington. It was characteristic of Robert that he could not keep his hands off other people's lives and always felt that he knew how to direct them for their own best interests. In his efforts to guide Carol he sometimes seemed unaware that his son had become a grown man and could not be treated as though he were still a minor. In spite of Robert's usual keen perception of other people's feelings he often seemed oblivious to the humiliations he caused Carol, who was still in part financially dependent on him.

Carol's difficulties came to a head early in October 1940, when Lillian was hospitalized after a serious operation. He visited her in the hospital one day and went home convinced that she was going

to die. She was in fact very ill, and Carol was too upset to remember that her gallant spirit had brought her through other critical illnesses and that the doctors had said she would recover. He called Robert, who, alarmed by his state, went immediately to South Shaftesbury to stay with Carol and his sixteen-year-old son, Prescott. When I saw Robert on his return, I found him in a very blue mood. He and Carol had spent one entire night talking, but Robert was sure that no suggestion he had made had altered Carol's thinking or convinced him that he was capable of any personal success. Four or five days later I was awakened by a call from Robert. He told me that Prescott had telephoned from the Stone House to say that his father, in the early hours of the morning, had shot himself. Robert asked me to meet him at the North Station in Boston and to go with him as far as Springfield, where he would be driven to South Shaftsbury. The train carried no parlor car in which we might have found privacy; we had to settle for a seat in the least crowded day coach. Robert talked and I listened. Later I discovered that an acquaintance of Robert's was sitting behind us and taking notes on the impetuous statements Robert made, in his grief, of how he had attempted to provide Carol with a life that would keep him secure and allow his abilities to flourish. The young man behind us was one of a number who attached themselves to Robert by claims that some of his older friends could not help finding dubious. They were for the most part younger people who tried to pursue careers in poetry and writing with an independence that bore some resemblance to Robert's own, but without his gifts. Robert could not find it in his heart to resist them. He never could see a lump of dough without thinking it could be made into a loaf of bread if only it were properly kneaded.

After Carol's death Robert brooded over the question of his failure to help his son accommodate to the world in which he lived. Robert's grief and his reflections on the disaster are best represented by a letter he wrote to Louis Untermeyer, one of the very few friends—if there was any other at all—to whom he would have confided in writing such expressions of his inmost feeling. "Dear Louis," he wrote:

> I took the wrong way with him. I tried many ways and every single one of them was wrong. Something in me is still asking for the chance to try one more. There's where the greatest pain is located. . . . You'll say it ought not to have come about that I should have to think for him. . . . I doubt if he rested from thinking day or night in the last few years. Mine was just an added touch to his mind to see if I couldn't make him ease up on himself and take life and farming off hand. I got humbled. . . . My manner will be intended to indicate henceforth that I acknowledge myself disqualified from giving counsel.

Despite this heartbroken disclaimer, Robert continued to give counsel— some of it, as his later life showed, even on an international scale.

During the year of Carol's tragedy, Robert negotiated the purchase of five acres of land adjacent to the Hervey Allen property in what was then part of Coconut Grove, now South Miami, in Florida. Next year, at Hervey's urging, he bought two prefabricated houses in the North and had them shipped down by rail to be assembled *in situ*. The purpose of this maneuver was to avoid the supposedly exorbitant costs extorted by Florida builders. As it turned out, the freight charges far exceeded any gouging he might have suffered. Robert had been familiar with Florida ever since he and Elinor had spent the winter of 1930 in Key West. The new houses at Coconut Grove were to provide a retreat and a center of operations for his annual escape from pneumonia, on land where he could raise gardenias, oranges, grapefruit, and avocados, where he could watch the painted buntings and their indigo cousins come and go and could hear the bob-whites whistle. The refuge was intended for Robert himself and had nothing directly to do with family problems, but it later turned out to be helpful to members of his family, notably when his grandson, Prescott, was working for his degree at the University of Miami.

As he did with Carol, Robert faced serious problems with his daughter, Irma. Always an individual going her own way, Irma did not readily fit into the pattern of family life. Unlike Lesley, who excelled in sports, Irma avoided games and walks on the Long Trail in Vermont, preferring to remain at home with her mother, where she could devote herself to fine handiwork with her needle and to her drawing. She, along with the other Frost children, were brought up under Robert's philosophy of hands-off as far as possible. But it was an erratic hands-off, inconsistent to say the least. In the larger decisions Robert and Elinor were extremely liberal in their policies, but one need read only a few of the family letters to see how much they involved themselves, almost identified themselves, with their children. While Irma was a student at Dana Hall in Wellesley it became obvious that she must have a special program, that the wear and tear of standard educational methods were not for her. Robert and Irma did not easily communicate, but his concern for her was as great as for her siblings. His way was to plan, to take action, always confident that he had found the right course. He found an opportunity when Irma, after her marriage to John Cone, turned up unannounced at South Shaftsbury with her infant son, declaring that she never would go back to the farm in Kansas where she had been living with her husband. When Robert saw that Irma's husband intended to follow her, he bought them a small poultry farm in North Bennington. On the failure of that venture, he used his influence at Yale to obtain for John a scholarship at the architectural school. John succeeded, and gained a fine position with a distinguished firm in Hanover, New Hampshire. Despite John's success, Irma was still threatening divorce, finding communication with her husband no easier than with her father. After Elinor's death, Irma did not make the journey to Gainesville, Florida, to be with her father, perhaps because of a deep-seated resentment toward him that outweighed his generous efforts to help.

It was in the summer of 1939 that I was asked by Robert to help him find a way of life for Irma, who by then had left her husband and with her younger son, Harold, was living in a small inn at Hanover. We found a possible refuge for them in the house then occupied by Mrs. Homer Noble, some three miles from the Homer Noble Farm in Ripton. A brook ran nearby and good neighbors were available for company. But in a short time friction developed, and again we had to move Irma and her boy, this time to a large dairy farm near Middlebury. Some time later, faced with the second failure after an auspicious beginning, Robert resorted to a scheme he had long thought of, which was to establish Irma in a small New England town where she might live, cultivate a garden, and be accepted as a kind of benevolent "village witch," in Robert's phrase. So, in the early spring of 1947, I made a list of real estate dealers, consulted the Boston papers daily for advertisements of houses for sale, preferably "North of Boston," and in the course of tracking them down, I drove Robert miles in all directions.

Finally we discovered what seemed the perfect answer, an attractive small house set back in a wooded lot on a quiet road in the town of Acton. A school was nearby. A fine country doctor had his office close at hand. An unusually lovely village green—with the proper white steeple, grocery store, and bank—was not ten minutes distant. Robert and Irma together bought the house. We all relaxed, and Robert particularly enjoyed the coincidence that brought Irma and the town of Acton together. Irma was a direct descendant through her grandfather of the White family, and ancestral Whites were among the "men of Acton" who in 1776 were present by "the rude bridge that arched the flood" in nearby Concord.

The dream was not to last. In mid-August, Robert's friend and lawyer, Erastus Hewitt, called the Homer Noble Farm to say that Irma had been found wandering on Brattle Street in Cambridge and taken to Robert's house. Dr. Merrill Moore warned that for her own safety she must be placed at once in a hospital. As soon as all who were concerned could meet at Brewster Street, Merrill drove us in a group to the State Hospital in Concord, New Hampshire, where he had already

R.F. in the Old Jewish Cemetery, Newport, Rhode Island, where in December 1959 he took part in a televised observance of Hanukah. He visited Touro Synagogue, founded 200 years before by Jews who came from Spain and Portugal to escape persecution. The synagogue was designated a National Historic Site in 1946.

Longfellow, whom R.F. deeply admired, wrote a poem about the cemetery. One stanza reads: *"And these sepulchral stones, so old and so brown,*
That pave with level flags their burial-place,
Seem like the Tablets of the Law, thrown down
And broken by Moses at the mountain's base."

(Ken Heyman)

made preliminary arrangements for Irma's admission. Merrill and Erastus drove back to Cambridge. Robert and I found rooms in a drummers' hotel in Concord. After a dreary night, Robert was put to the ordeal of going to the hospital and formally committing his daughter. Fortunately the confinement did not prove to be lasting. When Lesley returned from her duties for the State Department in Spain, she became Irma's guardian, and with great devotion and perspicacity worked out the ultimate solution for Irma's life. Lesley found rooms in a nursing home in northern Vermont where Irma can have her own furniture and possessions. A doctor is available but not present. Irma now lives a life of independence with only as much supervision as is indispensable.

His difficulties with Irma constituted the last of the family ordeals Robert was called on to face. Meanwhile, over the years, his barding around was leading him more and more to audiences beyond the bounds of the strictly academic. He appeared frequently at the Ford Hall Forum in Boston, which exposed him to an unassorted mass body of listeners and questioners. His last appearance there occurred the day before he entered the Peter Bent Brigham Hospital for his final illness. In October 1946, under the auspices of the Charles Phelps Taft Memorial Fund of the University of Cincinnati in Ohio, he gave a reading of the unpublished manuscript of *A Masque of Mercy*. On the first day of the Feast of Tabernacles, at the invitation of his longstanding friend, Dr. Victor E. Reichert, Rabbi of the Rockdale Avenue Temple in Cincinnati, he delivered a sermon in the Temple. In 1957 Robert took part in a series of programs sponsored by the Educational Television and Radio Center in Pittsburgh, Pennsylvania. In one of these programs Dr. Jonas Salk, developer of the Salk polio vaccine, discussed with Robert the similarities between science and poetry and the procedure the poet and the scientist must follow as well as the satisfaction both derived from fulfillment. The next year Dr. Salk wrote Robert a thank-you letter for a book Robert had sent him. In the last sentence of the letter—a revelation of the friendship the two men had reached—Dr. Salk quotes Robert back to himself, using words from Robert's essay-preface, "The Figure a Poem Makes," from his *Collected Poems* of 1939: "I did not realize," Salk writes, "although I often felt it so, that some of us in science do as you do in poetry. The moment of idea is always a moment of delight, and as we follow our inclination we reach wisdom which is discovery—or, as it may sometimes seem, disaster. The fear of this—the discovery that may undo delight—more often than we realize—keeps many from the discovery that 'ends in a clarification of life—not necessarily a great clarification . . . but a momentary stay against confusion'."

Such extensions of both the media through which he became familiar and the diversity of the audiences he addressed represent steps toward the culminating phase of Robert's career, in which he became a public figure in a far wider sense than he could have anticipated when he began "barding around."

73

IV

Public Life

To find that the utmost reward
Of daring should be still to dare.

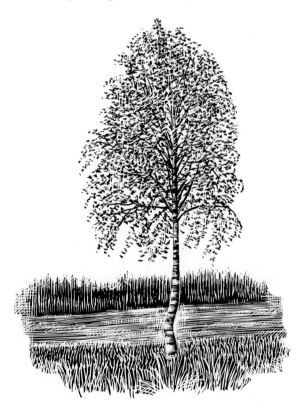

Both in his barding around and in the kind of public life that took him beyond lecturing and reading his poems, Robert inevitably exposed himself to misunderstanding and criticism. His interviews with the press and his relations with those with political power did not silence the accusation that he was adopting a mask or transforming himself into a popular legend. Even his friends were sometimes made uncomfortable by his willingness to indulge in pronouncements that had little to do with his poetry, and that seemed to vindicate those who suspected him of trying to create an image as a philosopher who advocated an American ideal of life out of tune with the modern world. Whatever the justice of these suspicions, two points must be remembered. One is Robert's consistent sense of confidence that he could direct other people's lives and, by extension, even the relations between one nation and another. The second is that his sense of participating in the highest order of decision was bred in him early, when as a child he was deeply affected by his father's political involvements in San Francisco. During the 1884 campaign to elect Grover Cleveland as president, Robert's father was active in the national contest as well as in his own campaign for the office of City Tax Collector. He used Robert as his errand boy, to go with him to the saloons where, according to what he told me, he won distinction for his ability to affix handbills to the wooden ceiling. The method: push a tack through the paper, toss paper and tack, with a silver dollar as backup, to the ceiling, and retrieve the dollar. He ate his noon meal with his father and the other men at the free-lunch counter. When Cleveland was elected, Robert celebrated by riding in the victory parade on top of a fire engine. Heady stuff for a boy of ten!

It seems inescapable that his childhood in San Francisco strengthened, if it did not actually cause, traits in his character that at least should be seen in perspective, however they may be judged. The relations between father and son, ranging as they did from a partnership in which the boy was assigned a questionably precocious role to outright physical cruelty when he gave offense or failed a mission, certainly had a lasting effect. By contrast, his mother was affectionately oversolicitous. Thus there existed a dichotomy unhealthy for a growing child. Robert was allowed to sell papers on the streets at the age of ten, but because of his fear of the dark he slept in his mother's room almost until his seventeenth year. His mother encouraged him to read such hero tales as *The Scottish Chiefs*, and did nothing to discourage the growth in him of a formidable ego. He frequently recalled her proud assertion "That Rob can do anything!" He used to tell me that as a boy living at the Abbotsford House, he often knelt in an armchair and, holding his hands over his ears, buried his face in the back of the chair to drown out the mysterious voices calling to him. The solicitude of his mother and the erratic behavior of his father could not help intensifying the stresses on a character which, through a combination of sensitiveness and genius, was born to stress no matter what. I am sure that more than a few persons would have tempered their impressions of Robert had they known of these early circumstances. It is true that he was jealous of other poets when their success seemed to exceed or threaten his own, but that is an almost unavoidable human weakness. He was quick to see enemies where like as not there were friends. He has been thought unfeeling toward his children, but if he suffered failures with them it was through misjudgment or overconfidence in his own wisdom, not through any lack of tenderness.

His contradictory upbringing may well go far to explain those "ructions" which Robert once admitted in a letter had the childish purpose of gaining his ends by making a nuisance of himself. Perhaps "nuisance" is too mild a word. After the death of Elinor, at the height of his despair, I was witness to the only public outburst of which I am aware. It was embarrassing. It was a repetition of his childhood tantrums, not in this case to gain any specific end but rather, in his mood of self-abasement and jealousy, to bolster his own ego. Like a bad boy he misbehaved during a lecture at Bread Loaf, and at the gathering afterward ruthlessly interrupted the reading by a visiting poet of a newly written play. In contrast to this public scene, I endured some private ones, always the result of a fancied slight to his dignity and always bringing on a similar reaction. More than once he made a childish escape into the woods around the Homer Noble Farm in the hope that we would believe him lost and would suffer accordingly. On one occasion, in a fit of rage, he began smashing a favorite chair. I told him he simply couldn't permit himself to break furniture. He answered that he could, and proceeded to finish the job. One of his not uncommon threats was to mix pills and swallow a dose that could have had a serious outcome. It took me time to learn how to deal with such situations. Unless there was real danger, as when during a winter visit to the farm he wandered off into the adjacent National Forest in snow up to his calves, I found the effective method was a calm neglect to comment on his behavior and an unobserved removal of obvious tools for destruction, whether an axe or a bottle of rum. I mention these incidents for the sake of truth, and also to emphasize that Robert suffered from a deep insecurity bred in him as a child, an insecurity that even invaded his deepest wish, the "ambition" (as he put it in his Introduction to E. A. Robinson's *King Jasper*) "to lodge a few poems where they will be hard to get rid of." I should add that the traits which to some seemed to cloud Robert's genius and reduce his personal stature did not grow more fixed with age. Instead, although they never entirely disappeared, with time they came less to the fore, becoming increasingly absorbed into the essential largeness of his nature.

Robert's public life, as I call it, was a combination of appointments held, official missions undertaken, and mounting recognition. These three elements are interwoven, and because it would be difficult to treat them as separate topics, I will deal with them chronologically.

In March 1950 he received recognition from a source that was

Both faces of
the Congressional
gold medal
voted to R.F.
by Congress
in 1960.

(Courtesy of
the Houghton
Library, Harvard
University)

neither literary nor academic. In tribute to what was erroneously be-
lieved to be his seventy-fifth birthday, the United States Senate passed
a resolution extending to Robert "the felicitations of the nation."
Four years later, under the misapprehension that he was being sent by
the State Department as a kind of ambassador of good will, he agreed to
accompany his daughter Lesley to a World Congress of Writers in Saõ
Paulo, Brazil. This was a considerable venture for a man of eighty,
unaccustomed to travel by air. It involved, as he said, "the longest
non-stop flight in the world," from Caracas in Venezuela to Rio de
Janeiro. In the course of the flight he learned that his presence had
been requested by the University at Saõ Paulo, but that the State
Department had at first held up the appointment, insisting that he
submit to an official briefing in Washington. With the help of President Eisenhower's assistant, Sherman Adams, Lesley had succeeded in
cutting through the obstructing red tape. On discovering that the
invitation had originated in Brazil, Robert wrote, "he flew more
lightly." He received a citation from the Brazilian Academy, and of that
occasion he later wrote with a characteristic mixture of pride and self-
doubt: "I responded not ungracefully. I begin to wonder about myself
if I may not have something after all." He goes on to speak of the crowd
that had listened to him in the Public Gardens at the Boston Arts
Festival and of the "distinguished treatment" he and Lesley received
from the ambassadors of both Brazil and Peru. "It sets me thinking
about being dazzled. But then there were the triumphs of Napoleon and
Vespasian . . ." Before he returned from Brazil to Vermont, he was
persuaded to make another spectacular flight, this time over the Andes
and Lake Titicaca to Lima in Peru. His reading there took place in the
midst of a street revolution that thinned his expected audience. He saw
the car of a Vargas official overturned and set on fire, but he did not
witness any shooting. He came back to the Homer Noble Farm with a
pocket full of semiprecious stones bought from the gypsies with the
aid of a former student. Appropriately set, they served as gifts to his
granddaughters and to friends.

79

(1) At R.F.'s 80th birthday party at the Lord Jeffrey Inn, Amherst.
(*Left to right*) President Charles Cole, Thornton Wilder, R.F., Archibald MacLeish,
Louis Untermeyer, Hyde Cox, Curtis Canfield. (Amherst College News Service)
(2) R.F. in conversation with Sherman Adams at Dartmouth College.

(Dartmouth College Archives)

During 1954 his eightieth birthday had been twice celebrated. His publishers, the firm of Holt, Rinehart and Winston, gave a party in his honor in New York, followed by what he later described as "a grueling three-hour session with nearly thirty reporters," during which he stood for the entire time "backed against the wall." The next night, with no sign of fatigue despite a hasty journey from New York to Amherst, he was honored by the college at the Lord Jeffrey Inn, where ninety friends and admirers gathered for dinner. To each guest Holt, Rinehart and Winston presented a copy of *Aforesaid,* a book containing Robert's own selection from his poems and specially printed for the occasion. Archibald MacLeish was the toastmaster; the speakers, President Charles Cole, Louis Untermeyer, and Thornton Wilder. A tribute by Robert's close friend, Professor George Whicher, whose sudden death had occurred three weeks earlier, was read by Professor Curtis Canfield. On behalf of a group of friends, Robert was presented with an Andrew Wyeth watercolor, "Winter Sunlight," by Edward Hyde Cox, of Crow Island, Manchester, and co-editor with Edward Connery Lathem of Robert's *Selected Prose*. This was the first public acknowledgment of a long and important friendship, which had begun in the thirties and continued until Robert's death. Over the years Hyde's house at Crow Island had become a place of refuge, where Robert found music, good conversation, and country walks. It was to Crow Island that Robert went on the day before he began his arduous trip to Russia, when he needed support in his resolution "still to dare."

In 1955 an act of the Vermont legislature officially bestowed the name Robert Frost Mountain on a local Ripton peak, modest enough and disappointingly invisible from his cabin, but welcome as a permanent stamp of his presence in one of his favorite regions.

Two years later occurred his triumphal visit to England and Ireland, mediated by another of the friends who were important in his life. When Sherman Adams was Governor of New Hampshire, he had attended a dinner in Frost's honor at the St. Botolph Club in Boston and surprised him by quoting lines from "New Hampshire." In 1956 Adams, by then Assistant to President Eisenhower, sent an emissary to Ripton to discover how his friend might feel about going to England on a mission of Anglo-American fellowship. Robert agreed to a visit in the spring of 1957. The response from England was immediate and more than gratifying. Oxford, Cambridge, and the National University of Ireland offered him degrees *honoris causa*. The Universities of London and of Manchester asked him to lecture. The University of Durham, which in 1951 had conferred an honorary degree on him *in absentia*, requested a visit in person. In a letter to Secretary of State John Foster Dulles, Robert asked that his times be planned for, that he not be "shot off as an unguided missile," and plans were duly coordinated.

Many friends volunteered their services as companion, but Lawrance Thompson, Robert's prospective biographer, arranged to meet him in London and help with his crowded schedule. Writing to Thompson of the coming journey, Robert said: "It will also sort of round off my rather great academic career in general. I have had about everything I can have in my own country. Now for the mother country. We are not talking of deserts. No triumphs for me. But satisfactions I dont see why I shouldnt be permitted." Among his fellow passengers on the plane crossing the Atlantic was Tallulah Bankhead. Reporters and cameramen in force met the plane when it landed, looking, as Robert supposed, for Tallulah, as indeed some of them were, but it was Robert who received the lion's share of attention by picture, interview, and B.B.C. broadcast.

Settled in his room at the Connaught Hotel, Robert slept for ten hours. He was to make his first official appearance the next day. In a letter strangely reminiscent of his earliest fears as a public speaker, he wrote: "With the first lecture this afternoon I'm scared much as of old in 1915-16-17-18-19-20-21-22—I don't remember when I began to be less than mortally scared. You have been let into the secret of why I like to make it out mortally. Its because I want to equal myself to the soldiers that went to face the bullets that I never faced—" Apparently he conquered his fears without the help of pebbles in his shoes or cold water on the back of his neck, for accounts of those who were present at the University of London spoke of a packed hall with a crowd of seven hundred whom "he never lost." F. S. Flint and T. S. Eliot confronted him from the third row.

At the University of Durham, Robert was delighted to be housed in the castle near the battlefield of Neville's Cross where David the Bruce, son of Robert's hero, Robert the Bruce, was defeated by the English. As he lay in the great canopied fourposter bed in the Bishop's room, Robert recalled his boyhood delight in Jane Porter's *The Scottish Chiefs,* and felt partly consoled for what he regarded as his failure at the dinner given him by the University. He feared that he had "rambled too much," feared that he was no longer scared enough to keep from being what he called "fatuous." But a stroll along the river beside the cricket fields and an evening at the house of Colleer Abbott, with good talk and his usual drink of Rose's lime juice spiked with rum and sweetened with two heaping spoonfuls of sugar, made him forget his concern. As Thompson escorted him home to the castle, Robert declared, "We'll never forget that night."

Back in London Robert spent two social days which included a cocktail party given him by Jonathan Cape, the British publisher, a party at which both C. Day Lewis and T. S. Eliot were present, and also a luncheon at the House of Lords. When Eliot, early in May, had learned of Robert's proposed visit to London, he had written in cordial anticipation of seeing and hearing him and had invited Robert to dine. Robert, who had not always been free from touchiness about the position Eliot occupied on the literary scene, wrote in answer: "It would be a great disappointment if my more or less official return to England

May Hill near Dymock, where R.F. walked with Edward Thomas and Jack Haines.

(Howard Sochurek, Life Magazine © Time Inc.)

didn't mean furthering our acquaintance; and I should be less a re-specter of persons than I am if I didn't hope to give you before I get through with this here world the highest sign of my regard." The renewal of his acquaintance with Eliot was one of the high-water marks of Robert's English visit.

Before he was to receive his Oxford degree, Robert paid a visit to Manchester, where he addressed the Manchester Luncheon Club, and another visit to Sussex to his old friend, John Squire. The latter proved to be an unrewarding call, of which Robert later wrote: "He wept more or less when we had to say good-bye. He was more unselfish in his day than I ever was. He threw himself away as if he didn't matter to himself . . . He's as total a sacrifice to Baccus as Edward Thomas was to war. And look at me in my calculated risks."

A risk, on whatever calculation or lack of it, promptly followed. Only two days before he was to receive his Oxford degree, Robert woke with a sore throat and sinus ache. As a precaution he regretfully canceled a planned visit in Berkshire to Edward Thomas's widow and her daughters, Bronwyn and Myfanwy. Instead he spent the day resting in bed, but to no avail. The throat became worse and the sinus pain more severe. Before resigning himself to a disturbed night, and always inclined to believe that you never could have too much of a good thing, he took two sleeping pills and two pain relievers that had been pre-scribed by his doctor before he began his journey. When Thompson called for him on Monday morning to prepare for the ride to Oxford, he found what he thought to be a very sick man. Determined to sum-mon a physician and puzzling how to avoid a confrontation with Robert, he excused himself and called the United States Embassy.

R.F. with
W.H. Auden
at Wadham
College gardens,
Oxford.

(Howard Sochurek,
Life Magazine
© Time Inc.)

R.F. entering
Oxford University
Divinity School
for the degree
ceremony
in June of 1957.

(Howard Sochurek,
Life Magazine
© Time Inc.)

Within minutes a young doctor came to the hotel. Armed with the fortunate information that the doctor came from Montana, Thompson opened the door to Robert's room, saying, "Here's a man from Willard's state." The reference to Robert's son-in-law may have mollified but did not deceive him. "Doctor, eh?" Robert asked. Larry was reassured by the examination that followed. Robert was overtired, had no fever, no congestion in his chest; he was reacting to the effects of two conflicting medicines, but he would be fully recovered in twenty-four hours. For safety's sake a doctor should check on his condition at Oxford, but there was no reason the journey should be postponed.

Delivered by the Embassy car, Robert, together with Thompson and Lesley Lee Francis, Robert's granddaughter, who had come from Spain for the occasion, were met by Sir Maurice Bowra, Warden of Wadham College and Robert's host. Thompson was relieved to learn from Sir Maurice that a physician had been alerted and that Robert's companion for the next days was to be his good friend Edward Connery Lathem, now Dean of Libraries and Librarian of Dartmouth College but at that time living on Boar's Hill while reading for his D. Phil. degree. With the scene set, Robert went to his splendid quarters in the Warden's Lodge, took a nap, and prepared for the dinner in his honor and the reception to follow.

The fourth of June 1957, when Robert was awarded his Oxford D. Litt., was more than a milestone in his career; it was, up to that moment, the apex of recognition. An Oxford convocation for the awarding of an honorary degree is short and formal and conducted wholly in Latin, with which Robert was thoroughly conversant. After being led to the Divinity Schools in formal procession, the degree recipient is brought from his place in the audience by the Public Orator, and— facing the Vice-Chancellor of the University, his back to the seated listeners—hears his citation and then receives his degree from the Vice-Chancellor, all this accompanied by many bows and much tipping of hats. Robert, in his gorgeous crimson and gray gown, heard himself proclaimed "a great poet" whose verse "with its echoes of Virgilian serenity has brought and will continue to bring unfailing consolation to a suffering world," and as one "devoted alike to the service of Ceres and the service of the Muses." Not everyone would choose "serenity" as a chief mark of Robert's poems, and his services to Ceres might have been questioned by a literate cow anchored at both ends, but it is hard not to imagine Robert repeating to himself on this occasion the line from Kipling he so often quoted to others: "I wish my mother could see me now."

Later in the afternoon Robert, still wearing his gown, read for an hour and a half to a packed house. Witnesses declared that he never talked better, never read better. Thompson closed his report to me with the capitalized words: "This was the high of the whole trip. IT WAS TUR-RIFFICK."

R.F. and
E.C. Lathem
at Oxford,
looking at the
honorary degree
awarded to
Henry Wadsworth
Longfellow.
"Ed, you're
the only friend
I've had who
has never been
a trial to me."

(Howard Sochurek,
Life Magazine
© Time Inc.)

R.F. looking at the stove and hob at Little Iddens, Dymock, in 1957.

(Howard Sochurek, Life Magazine © Time Inc.)

After a night of partying, Robert talked next day to the Rhodes Scholars, and, following lunch with Lord and Lady Beveridge, returned to Wadham to pack for his journey into the Cotswolds. Sir Maurice asked Robert as a personal favor to permit the doctor to make sure he was fit to take on the proposed visit to Gloucestershire. The doctor found little wrong except the remains of the cold Robert had caught in London and the fatigue, inevitable in a man of his years, resulting from the strenuous program he had undertaken. As a way of thanking the doctor, who as an agent of the National Health Service could not charge a fee, Robert gave him an autographed copy of his poems into which he had tucked a five-pound note. The doctor riffled the pages, discovered the note, shut the book promptly, pointed a forefinger as if at a child, said, "Naughty, naughty!" and quickly left the room.

The drive to Gloucestershire scarcely allowed Robert time to compose himself for renewed memories of his days at Beaconsfield and Dymock with Elinor and his children, a sojourn that had brought him his first notable success as a poet through the publication of *A Boy's Will*. He asked to sit alone with the driver, leaving in the back

A moment's diversion at Dymock in 1957.

(Howard Sochurek, Life Magazine © Time Inc.)

Approaching Little Iddens, Dymock, 1957.

(Howard Sochurek, Life Magazine © Time Inc.)

seat Lee, Thompson, and the Time-Life team of Miss Beatrice Dobie (as narrator) and Howard Sochurek (as photographer). Of this journey Robert wrote: "I go with the sporting events boys from *Life* who are making an expedition to Leadington, Little Iddens, Ryton, and Jack Haines (now in Cheltenham) to write me up and photograph me farming in the days that are no more." One needs only to look at Sochurek's pictorial record in this book to realize that memories happy in themselves came back to Robert with the pain of loss. In his first biographical volume, *The Early Years,* Thompson treats fully those days spent in the Dymock region with the Georgian poets Lascelles Abercrombie, Wilfrid Gibson, William Henry Davies, and, most important of all, Edward Thomas. A significant background contribution to the story is *Dymock through the Ages* by the Reverend Eric Gethyn-Jones, now a Canon of Bristol Cathedral and Chaplain at Berkeley Castle, who at the time of Robert's 1957 visit was serving as Vicar at Dymock. In 1971 Ted and I had the great pleasure of visiting the Gethyn-Joneses and being taken to Little Iddens where on the site of Robert's old vegetable garden a rust-eaten horseshoe had just been turned up by a plow. It now rests on the cabin mantlepiece at the Homer Noble Farm.

Before receiving his degree at Cambridge, Robert returned to London for further festivities and meetings with old friends. He had already made a preliminary visit to Cambridge on May twenty-third, when Basil Willey, as a Fellow of Pembroke College, entertained him at tea and escorted him to a sherry party in his honor. During this visit, Robert again read to an overflow audience with an éclat that reportedly exceeded even his reception in London. When the day came for the award of the degree, the ceremony paralleled the occasion at Oxford in its ritual and the respect it showed him. Lord Tedder as Chancellor made the award, and the Deputy Orator read the citation in a Latin whose academic wit managed gracefully to allude to Hesiod, to quote Robert's beloved Horace, to recall the preeminent friendship of his life with Edward Thomas, and to recognize some of the primary qualities of Robert's poems. To paraphrase in English: "Many poets, few farmers, have praised the country," the citation begins. "This man deeply knows what he sings, the works and days of his acres . . . Here is the life of the Sabines, the song of Ascra [birthplace of Hesiod]. But there is in it no Boeotian fat or rusticity; rather a sage and almost Stoic judgment of things. How living those dialogues! 'Good fences make good neighbors.' [In Latin, for the curious: 'Ubi boni limites, ibi boni vicini']." The citation goes on to describe the poems as "speaking in altogether everyday language" in which the reader nonetheless recognizes "the Muses' gift." Finally: "As a visitor he once lived in the English countryside, friend of Edward Thomas and other poets, when he first gained admirers of the poems in which New England breathes. Soon famous in his own land he has for forty years been esteemed and honored by both peoples." Surviving the taxing formalities of the occa-

(1) Cambridge University, England.
The procession to the Senate House for the awarding of the honorary degree.

(Howard Sochurek, Life Magazine © Time Inc.)

(2) R.F. signs the National University Register after receiving the D. Litt (Honoris Causa).
Watching is Eamon DeValera, Chancellor of the University
and Prime Minister of Ireland.

(Wide World Photos)

sion, during which, as Mrs. Ivor Richards wrote me from Cambridge, he was "very much himself and ruggedly ready to carry through the whole program," Robert put in a night's sleep at the University Arms Hotel and returned to London.

The next important engagement on Robert's calendar brought to mind an incident in the early days at the Homer Noble Farm, when we all gathered for supper around a yellow oak table. One evening Robert telephoned his friend Louis Untermeyer, who was living at that time in Elizabethtown, New York. Learning that the Untermeyers were away from home, he carried on a ten-minute conversation in brogue with the Irish maid, Delia, sounding as though he had emigrated from Ireland a fortnight before. As the children showed their delight, he became more and more the actor. I have a letter written in 1960 that gives further evidence of his predilection for the Irish:

> They tell me the Irish have it and we have become an Irish country not to say an Irish Catholic country . . . I have seen it ahead ever since I had Maude Gonne's friend, Katy O'Keefe, for my teacher of English history in the Lawrence High School in 1888 and got only 98 for my work because I had to confess I was probably wrong in my attitude toward James Second. Earlier than that even I had caught in the city of Lawrence an accent of Arah from off the streets that bothered my mother. And you must have noticed how naturally I take to the Irish Jesuits and they to me. One of my best evenings was with them at Holy Cross on how there was more religion outside the church than in the church, namely saints that come to trouble and refresh the church.

R.F. and Carl Sandburg with Quincy Mumford, Librarian of Congress.

(Courtesy of the Library of Congress)

When the National University of Ireland invited him to accept the degree of D. Litt. *honoris causa* on June nineteenth, Robert felt as though he had come full circle. It was therefore a tired but happy man who, with Thompson, crossed the Irish Channel to keep the engagement. Relieved of his fears that he might fail his audiences in England, he went as a schoolboy on a holiday. His good friends Jack and Moira Sweeney, with whom he had spent happy hours in Boston, had built themselves a beautiful house at Corofin in County Clare, on a height that looked toward distant hills beyond a lake where wild swans bred. They met Robert, provided him with a car and driver, and saw him to University College in Dublin, where Moira's brother-in-law, Michael Tierney, was Provost. Robert stayed with the Tierneys, and particularly admired, perhaps with a tinge of envy, their six thriving sons. How had the Tierneys raised them so successfully? Was it inheritance, upbringing, perhaps religion? Robert never stopped asking the question. His drives and picnics with the Tierneys and Sweeneys were experiences he did not forget. The degree ceremony and the talk he gave as part of the occasion were high points in his tour. So his mission and his adventure came to an end, and on June twenty-first he flew with Thompson from Shannon back to Boston.

94

Appointed Consultant in Poetry to the Library of Congress in 1958, Robert was interviewed in December by the columnist Mary McGrory. "In the scant two months he has been here," she wrote, "Robert Frost has caught a slight case of Potomac Fever. He would like to stay here in elective office." This was witty and perceptive, but suggested no knowledge of Robert's boyhood background in the politics of California. It seems inescapable, as I have indicated, that his confidence in his ability to direct other people's lives, and his extension of that belief into national affairs, was bred in the bone and not acquired by contagion in Washington. At eighty-two, with four Pulitzer prizes to his credit, ten books, a mission to Brazil, and a triumphant visit to four British and one Irish university, he accepted the call to Washington as an adventure. A little tired of the old, he sought a new field. Thinking of what remained of his life, he used to say: "The rest I give to pleasure," meaning not sybaritic but intellectual pleasures. During his first year as Consultant in Poetry, Robert paid two official visits to the Library, in May and in October, and made frequent informal calls as well. In 1959 he became Consultant in the Humanities, and continued to serve under that title until his death. He was supplanted as Consultant in Poetry by a resident poet who could give to the office the time and attention to detail it demanded.

Robert's headquarters were in the Poetry Room high up in the Library with a view of the Capitol. His assistant, Miss Phyllis Armstrong, proved a devoted guide through the complexities of bureaucracy. Each of his visits was marked by a reading in the Coolidge Auditorium and a series of small teas in the Poetry Room, where he entertained friends of the Library and old acquaintances such as the Gardner Jacksons, the William Shafroths, the Francis Biddles, the Felix Frankfurters, and Senator and Mrs. Ralph Flanders. A large cocktail party in the Whittall Pavilion was also a regular feature of his visits. Luncheons with the Library staff and distinguished visitors enlivened his days and at times brought terror to Library officials, fearful of a too sharp encounter with Carl Sandburg or of indiscretions that might affect Congressional votes at budget time. His interviews with the press, many of them recorded in Edward Connery Lathem's *Interviews with Robert Frost*, brought to public attention a side of Robert that was new to many readers. The interviews, as Lathem says, "present Mr. Frost informally, sometimes casually, yet always in the character of a performer—for performance was ever at the heart of what he aspired to as artist and man."

True words, but Robert also had a deep hankering for something more than masterful performance. In his early days as Consultant, he once described himself as "Poet in Waiting." Though he did not say explicitly what he was waiting for, it was undoubtedly in part the opportunity to participate at a high level in active affairs. In May 1960 he went before a subcommittee of the Senate to plead for the establishment of a National Academy of the Arts, espousing what he called "passionate preference" for the arts and for the pursuit of excellence in general. Meanwhile he was meeting with members of Congress at informal evening sessions at the home of Representative Stewart Udall, sessions at which talk ranged over wide areas from politics to poetry. Becoming what he called "easy in harness," he had begun to feel the pleasure of closeness to "these great affairs," as he phrased it. He was readying himself for further participation in public life.

He had already taken advantage of one opportunity to intervene in a public cause, in this case a legal action. The American-born poet, Ezra Pound, indicted by the United States for treason for his broadcasts in Italy during World War II, had been adjudged incompetent to stand trial and confined in St. Elizabeth's Hospital in Washington. By 1958 his confinement had lasted thirteen years. Robert's relations with Pound had been uneasy, to say the least, ever since they had first met in the Poetry Bookshop in London during Robert's first English sojourn. Robert did not share the veneration for Pound's poetry that prevailed overwhelmingly in the literary world. He even mistrusted the influence Pound had used to promote the publication of Robert's own poems in America. To Robert's strong vein of patriotism Pound's utterances during the war were abhorrent. Yet he wholeheartedly joined in the efforts initiated and carried on by Archibald MacLeish, Ernest Hemingway, T. S. Eliot, and Pound's American publisher, James Laughlin, to secure Pound's release from St. Elizabeth's Hospital. If Robert was a latecomer in the campaign and the spade work had been done by others, his intervention was nonetheless effective in tipping the scales at the critical moment. In 1957, after his return from his English tour, Robert agreed to go with MacLeish to Washington for a conference with Attorney General William P. Rogers, who had expressed a wish to meet with the principal participants in the campaign. Robert and MacLeish duly met with those whom Robert always referred to as "the boys at the Department of Justice," but without making progress. Political as well as literary influences were presently brought to bear, and by early April of 1958 the situation had reached a point, in Lawrance Thompson's words, in which "all that was needed was a prominent figure to cut through the red tape . . ." At MacLeish's instigation, Robert went again to Washington, found Attorney General Rogers receptive, and on the advice of William Shafroth, a legal expediter for the government, asked Thurman Arnold to take Pound's case. Arnold not only took it, but declined to charge any fee. Arnold drew up a document for Robert to sign and submit as *amicus curiae* to the District Court. Robert took the proposed draft back to his hotel where he spent a sleepless night trying to reduce it to his own words and emphasis. As the sun rose he fell asleep, satisfied at last. His memorable statement, as finally submitted to the court, has been published in *Robert Frost: Poetry and Prose,* edited by Edward Connery Lathem and Lawrance Thompson, and also in a note in Thompson's *Selected Letters.* As he wrote in his page-and-a-half plea, he rested his case on the verdict

R.F. reciting "The Gift Outright" at J.F.K.'s inauguration.
"Every time Robert Frost comes to town the Washington Monument stands up a little straighter."
—James Reston in The New York *Times*

(George Silk, Life Magazine © Time Inc.)

by Dr. Winfred Overholser, the Superintendant of St. Elizabeth's Hospital, "that Ezra Pound is not too dangerous to go free in his wife's care, and too insane ever to be tried . . ." Yet as if not really satisfied with such a disposition by law alone, he continued: "There is probably legal procedure to help toward a solution of the problem. But I should think it would have to be reached more by magnanimity than by logic and it is chiefly on magnanimity I am counting." Magnanimity was a favorite theme with Robert, and the word would echo again in the Crimea during his interview with Khrushchev. If Robert was inclined to take excessive credit for his part in the campaign to free Pound, his impulsive elation may be one more reflection of his early days in San Francisco and the fascination with power and politicking that they bred in him.

To millions of television viewers Robert's presidentially invited appearance at the inauguration of John F. Kennedy was something of a heroic feat. They saw an old man, his hair tossed by the wind, struggling—against brilliant sunshine reflected from untimely snow, with eyes in which cataracts were already developing—to read the poem he had written for the occasion. They saw Vice President Lyndon B. Johnson gallantly try to shade Robert's manuscript with his tall silk hat, only to make matters worse by plunging the pages into deep shadow. They saw Robert put aside his prepared poem, and heard him recite his capsule summary of American history, "The Gift Outright," in a strong, clear voice, triumphing over circumstances by which he might well have been completely daunted. But the days preceding this courageous spectacle, days through which it was my part to shepherd him, produced a comedy of errors which it would be a pity not to record.

Robert and I arrived in Washington by train in midafternoon on January eighteenth, 1961. Neither I nor our astonished porter anticipated the reception we were to receive. Robert stepped from the car to be met by Stewart Udall, newly appointed Secretary of the Interior. Behind him, in full-dress uniform, stood a Marine Corps major, and behind him two other marines in command, not of ordinary porter's carts, but two cagelike structures on wheels into which they put our solitary suitcases, one in each cage. Evidently we were not living up to sartorial expectations. Major Bruce Meyers—Robert's designated aide for the inauguration, as we learned—led us to a large black limousine, and we were driven off in style. Before delivering me to the Jefferson Hotel, Major Meyers handed me a card on which were written Robert's address and a telephone number that was supposed to reach him. The address read 3509 K Street. The house where Robert was to stay belonged to a prominent Democratic committeewoman, who had cajoled or compelled her Republican tenant, Senator Kenneth Keating, into making a more precipitate move than he relished so that she could make room for inaugural guests. Robert was delighted by his quarters and by the breakfast stores with which Mrs. Udall had thoughtfully

R.F. shakes hands with former President Eisenhower at the inauguration of John F. Kennedy.

(George Silk, Life Magazine © Time Inc.)

stocked the refrigerator. He was under the impression that he was to be the sole occupant of the house. Robert settled in for a rest before attending a dinner in Georgetown given by Walter Lippmann, at which former President Truman was also a guest. At the Jefferson I was preparing myself for a solitary dinner downstairs when I heard a knock at my door. I opened it expecting a maid or a messenger boy and was surprised to find Major Meyers instead. He gave me a new card correcting Robert's address to M Street, but not mentioning any change of telephone number.

After a reunion luncheon at the Library of Congress next day, a light snow began to fall. We were shipped to our various addresses in the Library car, and I repeated to the driver Robert's address — 3509 M Street. After I was dropped at the Jefferson, Robert was taken on toward Georgetown, but whether because of the original confusion about the address, or because of fatigue on Robert's part, or because of the already thickening snow, the driver failed to find the house where Robert was quartered. The car circled through one street and another until Robert luckily recognized a familiar landmark and was belatedly deposited. He went in to rest; perhaps he dozed, but I suspect he tinkered with the poem he was to deliver on the morrow. Meanwhile the storm developed into a blizzard. The District of Columbia was unskilled in dealing with its infrequent snows. Scarcely a car had chains or snow tires. Traffic was quickly reduced to chaos.

This was Thursday, and the inaugural concert had been scheduled for the evening. We had planned a small family dinner at the Jefferson for Robert, his grandson Prescott, and Prescott's wife Phyllis, who were to come in their car prepared to drive us to Constitution Hall. Alarmed by the strength of the storm, I called Robert in Georgetown at the number given me by Major Meyers. At first no answer, then a gruff voice announcing, "Senator Keating on the wire." I apologized and rang off, somewhat dismayed, but thinking that the storm and the influx of inaugural visitors had thrown the telephone service out of gear. I dressed and went to the lobby to await Robert's arrival. I watched an endless chain of hotel guests coming in with snow-covered bags. The white marble floor at the entrance became a soggy puddle of melting snow. Still no Robert. Lawrance Thompson came from his hotel around the corner to find me shivering. We went to the bar and had a drink. Meanwhile it had become obvious that something unusual was going on. Waiters carrying trays hurried back and forth. Service at the bar was growing haphazard. We looked into the dining room and saw unwonted disorder, tables half set or not completely cleared. In a far corner of the almost empty room a disconsolate Van Cliburn, the prospective soloist of the evening, sat watched by his apprehensive mother. Foiled at every attempt to reach Robert by telephone, and informed that the concert had been canceled, Larry and I had another drink. In final desperation we went to the dining room and out of the melée managed to obtain two cups of hot soup, which we took to our observation post in the lobby. At last Robert, Prescott, and Phyllis arrived in what was probably the only car in the District wearing chains. They had experienced no driving trouble themselves, but had been constantly held up by lines of stalled cars.

Hopefully we went to the dining room, and were cheered by the sight of a well-known patron of the Jefferson, the entertainer Victor Borge, who with the hotel manager was serving the few diners with Cornish Rock game hens from Borge's own farm. They had been taken from the Jefferson freezer lockers and cooked in the kitchen by Borge himself. The Frost family departed almost immediately after dinner so that Robert could have a good night's sleep before the inauguration next day. Robert left with Larry and me his last revision of his inaugural poem, which was to be a prelude to his reading of "The Gift Outright," so that I could make a fair copy for Stewart Udall, who had offered to have a transcript prepared in the morning on President Eisenhower's large-letter typewriter. Late into the night, on the only typewriter available in the hotel, Larry and I worked in the staff dining room while the winds howled outside.

When Robert reached Georgetown, he firmly bolted all the doors in the house. Stewart Udall's mother and sister had spent the previous night there, and Robert, austere as he was to the point of suspicion about such female proximity, and fearful also of a raid on his breakfast milk and egg in the refrigerator, took what he considered appropriate action. His precautions had an unexpected result. When Major Meyers arrived at Georgetown in the morning to take Robert to the inauguration, he got no response to his ringing of the bell, and the bolted doors defied his key. Not for nothing had he been trained as a marine. He somehow scaled the wall of the house and got in through an unlocked window. I learned of this episode through indirect sources. Robert never mentioned it to me or to Larry, never disclosed his feelings when he found himself face to face with the major in full-dress uniform, white gloves and all.

Inaugural day was clear and cold, with deep snow all about. Larry and I made our way to the Capitol grounds where we found our reserved seats on the benches in front of the official platform. Lesley and her family, Robert's granddaughter Robin Hudnut and her husband, and the Prescott Frosts with their children had already taken their places, their feet firmly planted in eight inches of snow. After the ceremony, the Frosts moved on to a lunch snack and later to their seats for the inaugural parade. Larry and I, without seats and emotionally exhausted, returned to the Jefferson for a warming drink and a club sandwich. We began to worry about Robert. After lunch at the Capitol he was to ride in the parade to the President's box in the reviewing stand. He would have had a long day, and the cold was intense. Could he unaided free himself from the presidential box and retire to the warmth of the Georgetown house without waiting for the end of the parade? We made our way on foot to Pennsylvania Avenue, hoping to get near enough to the reviewing stand to discover whether he was still there. We could not see him. At the Jefferson again, we telephoned Robert's supposed number and were greeted by the irate voice of Senator Keating telling us in no uncertain terms that he had reached the end of his patience and wanted no more of this man Frost. Not long after, the telephone rang in my room and I heard Robert's voice coming at me in mixed tones of rage and sorrow. How could we have left him without a telephone call to cheer him in his usual postperformance doubts? I told him of our efforts and of Senator Keating's response, and at this point the mystery began to clear. Senator Keating had taken his established telephone number with him when he changed his address, and a new line had hastily been installed in the Georgetown house where Robert was quartered. Unfortunately this line worked only for outgoing calls; all incoming calls went to Senator Keating. Somewhat mollified when we got the telephone difficulties ironed out, Robert agreed to take a nap and join us for dinner with members of his family before going to the Armory ball, where he had a box.

The ride to the Armory seemed everlastingly slow. Bumper to bumper we crept along rutted and snow-choked streets. When we finally reached our goal we could not get near a cleared space. The banks of snow presented a problem to those of us in long skirts and slippers, but with the help of strong-armed policemen we made a successful crossing. Through the dancing crowd we traversed the Armory floor, by now thoroughly wet, to Robert's box. Robert and Lesley were duly posted in front to receive greetings from the floor. I stationed myself at the back to serve as combined receptionist and forager. Larry and Prescott were told off to procure champagne. They came back triumphant in their first attempt, but their second found the larder bare. Meanwhile a steady stream of visitors called, some old friends, some newer acquaintances or complete strangers who wanted to shake Robert's hand. The arrival of the young President and his strikingly beautiful wife marked, for most onlookers, the climax of the occasion, a symbol of Robert's hope for "A golden age of poetry and power," as he put it in the poem he was unable to read in the glare of sunlight and snow.

The ball over and Robert's grandchildren dispersed, Lesley, Lee, Larry, Robert, and I were left to make our way out. It dawned on us that through some oversight no transportation had been provided for us. As we made slow headway toward the door, it suddenly became obvious that Robert had taken all he could bear. I saw a uniformed officer, whom I mistook for a policeman, and asked his help in clearing our exit and finding a cab. No cabs were available, but my policeman turned out to be a fire chief, who offered to drive us in his truck. Meanwhile a passerby, overhearing our conversation, came to our rescue, generously proposing to deliver us all to our separate destinations in his station wagon. Larry accompanied Robert to Georgetown to make sure that all was well in the house and to try to reassure his doubts so that he could have an untroubled night's rest. Larry had to walk through the snow all the way back from Georgetown to his Washington hotel in his dancing pumps!

Through the good offices of Thomas Winship of the *Boston Globe,* who was in Washington during the inauguration, Robert was invited to call on the President on Sunday morning at eleven o'clock. I accompanied him past the deserted stands to the White House, and when Robert was immediately escorted to the private family quarters, I seated myself downstairs and prepared for an extended wait. Not long after an usher came to tell me that Mrs. Kennedy had asked that I be brought upstairs. I was shown into her bedroom, where she sat propped in a canopied four-poster amidst a spread of Sunday newspapers. Robert sat in a small rocking chair near the foot of the bed. The President brought me a chair and seated me on Mrs. Kennedy's left. Robert, completely at ease, settled in for a bout of the kind of talk he always relished, showing no visible consciousness that it would have to come to an end within a reasonable time. Presently the telephone rang by Mrs. Kennedy's bed. I overheard her say, "No, not now. Mr. Frost is here. A little later." Suspecting that the call had to do with her lunch tray, and aware that she was still recovering from the birth of her son John, I began to wonder how I could hint to Robert that we should leave. I had failed to remind him before we came that as guest of honor he should make the first move. (If I had done so, he would have forgotten.) Deciding that I had to be the one to act, I rose, thanked Mrs. Kennedy, gave Robert a look, and moved to the door. The President followed me, and I found myself standing with him by the elevator. I could still hear the rise and fall of Robert's voice. What could I talk about? Conversation in the bedroom had centered on our historical past. I said I wished I knew more about American history, that it was Scottish history I had read when I was growing up in Edinburgh and Stirling. My impulse was rewarded. The President loved Scottish history; it was full of deeds and heroes. By the time Robert had finally said his farewell, we were discussing Robert's own early favorite, Jane Porter's *The Scottish Chiefs.* Escorted by President Kennedy, we left the White House. Next day Robert left for his annual visits to Agnes Scott College and the University of Georgia; from there he would go on to his five acres in South Miami for a well-deserved rest.

In March 1961, as Lecturer on the Samuel Paley Foundation, Robert flew to Israel, where he was to spend ten days as a guest of the Hebrew University in Jerusalem. With him again as companion was Lawrance Thompson. Driven from New York to the airport at Idlewild in the Mayor's bubble-top car, in the company of his daughter Lesley and a group of friends, he was delighted to learn of the quotation from the Old Testament book of Exodus which El Al had inscribed in Hebrew behind its ticket counter, reading, in the King James version, "I bare [carried] you on eagle's wings." It was reassuring. Unfortunately Robert's eagle developed mechanical troubles before take-off. Passen-

R.F. lecturing in the auditorium of Hebrew University. "Poetry is a way of taking life by the throat."

(David Rubinger, Jerusalem)

gers were returned to a kind of banquet room where Robert, who had already dined well, had to spend two hours toying with what was called "an eight course dinner." It was not an auspicious start, but he was no longer an inexperienced traveler aloft and had learned to keep his fears in abeyance as he developed his "air legs."

In Israel Robert faced a demanding program, which included two lectures, two so-called talking sessions, a reception, a large luncheon, and many informal meetings with members of the university faculty. In between official engagements, he enjoyed sightseeing in Jerusalem and an overnight trip to Beersheba and Ashkelon. In the course of a visit to Haifa, he was able to inspect the Caesarea and the Beth Shearim excavations. On his way to Tel Aviv, where he was to make a final appearance under the joint auspices of the Tel Aviv branch of the university and the United States Embassy, he stopped at Nazareth.

R.F. with Lawrance Thompson and a guide standing by the walls of Jerusalem

(Harold Howland)

Summing up the Israeli sojourn, Thompson wrote that Robert's talks were "fabulously successful and the warmth of the Israeli hospitality touching . . . he left there loving everybody."

From Israel, Robert and Thompson flew to Athens, where Robert had promised Charles Rice, a friend with Middlebury College connections, to speak at Athens College. Housed at the American Embassy, Robert once again was feted. He attended a large reception at the Embassy and was given a party by the National Society of Greek Writers at which he and Stephen Spender exchanged toasts. He did not miss the opportunity to climb the Acropolis, and went one evening with friends to view it by floodlight.

Leaving Athens on March twenty-fifth, Robert and Thompson flew to London, where a succession of festivities had been planned in recognition of Robert's eighty-seventh birthday. These included a

(1) At Hebrew University, Jerusalem, R.F. views the Dead Sea Scrolls with Bernard Cherrick, Executive Vice-chairman of the Hebrew University's Board of Governors.

(American Friends of the Hebrew University)

(2) R.F. in the Meah Shearim market of the ultra-orthodox quarter of Jerusalem tries a banana.

(Harold Howland)

(3) A session with students of the Hebrew University. "I'll rumple their brains fondly. I'll give two lectures and sit around with students."

(American Friends of the Hebrew University)

luncheon given by United States Ambassador David Bruce, a visit to King's College, Cambridge, a dinner at which the poet Day Lewis was host, a dinner at the House of Lords, and another at the Greek Embassy given by the poet-Ambassador, George Seferis. Whether Robert was able to keep all of the engagements planned for him I do not know. I have no records of my own, for while he was abroad Ted and I, together with my sister and brother-in-law, had driven south for a delayed vacation. I do know that Robert came home sooner than he was expected, because the return trip of our vacation party was punctuated by telegrams and telephone calls urging me to hurry home and make my peace with a very tired man.

One final thrust into public life, this time truly close to the highest sources of power, remained to Robert before the end. It was a thrust that he was almost prevented from making by a nearly fatal attack of pneumonia in February of 1962 while he was enjoying his annual retreat to "Pencil Pines," his refuge in South Miami, Florida. After his recovery a month later, he said in an interview with a reporter from *The Miami Herald:* "I thought I was going to die the other day. . . . Then I thought again, that I'd stay around and see who wins the next election." He did not live to see the next election. He did live to accept President Kennedy's invitation to go to Russia. This was a mission that brought out several fascinating sides of his nature, all with roots in his earliest days: a certain innocence, an aspiration toward high-mindedness, a habit of judging even the greatest affairs by his own internal measure, a confidence again in his power to direct others and solve their problems, accompanied by a failure to see that in using a personal opportunity for what he considered magnanimous ends he was at least in part being used by others with different ends in view. Whatever the strength or vulnerability of these traits, his Russian trip represented the utmost enlargement, in his last years, of elements in him that have sometimes been thought parochial or chauvinistic or narrowly conservative.

The Russian visit has become a well-documented story. Frederick B. Adams, Jr., who went with him to Moscow, has described at first hand, in a small volume privately printed for the Club of Odd Volumes in Boston, his meetings with Russian literati, his enthusiastically received readings, his mixed pleasure in the company of the poet Yevtushenko, his delight in a visit to the dacha at Peredelkino where another poet, Chukovsky, had established in his garden a library for children. Franklin Reeve, who also accompanied Robert as his interpreter, was personally present at his climactic interview with Khrushchev and has recorded their conversation in *Robert Frost in Russia,* published by the Atlantic Monthly Press. Stewart Udall, in an article written for the *New York Times Magazine,* has recapitulated the story and supplied pertinent comments on the developing Cuban missile crisis which was going on at the time, a crisis of whose full import Robert could not have been aware.

The dais at R.F.'s 88th birthday dinner at the Pan American Union in Washington in 1962 included Chief Justice and Mrs. Earl Warren; Justice Felix Frankfurter; Adlai Stevenson; the Dean of the Diplomatic Corps, the Ambassador of Nicaragua; Secretary of the Interior Stewart Udall and his wife; Mr. and Mrs. Robert Penn Warren; Mr. and Mrs. Mark Van Doren; R.F.; and his publisher at Holt, Rinehart and Winston, Alfred C. Edwards and Mrs. Edwards.

"I've had the same publisher for thirty-five years and those fellows there who have been my editors . . . they all have been friends of poetry; they've been my kind of man."

(National Park Service, Abbie Rowe)

It was in May 1962, while Robert was on duty at the Library of Congress, that Stewart Udall arranged a dinner meeting for him with Anatoly Dobrynin, the Soviet Ambassador to the United States. Conversation at this dinner went so well that Udall asked the Ambassador to discover whether it would be possible to plan a "cultural exchange" between Robert and a Russian poet. Dobrynin enthusiastically agreed, and with the approval of our State Department, the scene was set. President Kennedy sent Robert a formal invitation. Robert wrote in reply: "How grand of you to think of me in this way and how like you to take the chance of sending anyone like me over there affinitizing with the Russians . . ." He had earlier written to Udall: "How brotherly it all seems. By the accident of our falling in friendship with you and Lee [Mrs. Udall] we have been brought out on top of a new pinnacle

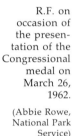

R.F. on occasion of the presentation of the Congressional medal on March 26, 1962.

(Abbie Rowe, National Park Service)

of view that makes me for one feel dangerously like a monarch of all fifty states I survey." With these thoughts in mind, Robert set out with Fred Adams and Frank Reeve for Moscow on the same plane as Secretary Udall, who was embarking on a technological mission with a group of hydroelectric engineers.

From the onset of his Russian journey, Robert had set his heart on a personal interview with Premier Khrushchev, but throughout the early part of his visit it seemed that he was to be disappointed. This prospective defeat of his principal hope contributed to his mounting fatigue and sickness. Then came an occasion that seemed only to confirm an unfavorable outcome to his suspense. Robert was to take part in a Soviet television recording of his sojourn. Before this could occur, Fred Adams learned that Stewart Udall planned to fly to Gagra

A
picture
of a
Russian birch
sent to R.F.
in September
of 1962
from
Frieda Lurie
and Elena
Romanova,
who acted as
his guides in
the U.S.S.R.
"Dear Mr. Frost:
We have
something
in common
after all,
haven't we?"

in the Crimea for an interview with Khrushchev early the next morning. Both Adams and Reeve realized that this news would be an inconsolable blow to Robert; he would feel worse than neglected, he would feel that he had been run out on. They decided not to tell Robert at once, hoping to get a message to Udall on the plane, but the messenger arrived after the plane had taken off. The news had to be broken no matter what the consequences. Reeve tried first, only to be abruptly dismissed after a minute or two. Adams made a second effort to see whether he might have better success, but was greeted with the words, "Don't you preach to me, Fred Adams!" Robert shut himself in his room alone, emerging half an hour later to face the television cameras as planned and to score another triumphal appearance. Later that night, at the house of Jack Matlock, the cultural attaché at our Embassy, Robert had his reward. A telephone call came through to say that he was to fly to Gagra at eight the next morning and meet with Premier Khrushchev.

As they returned to his hotel after dinner with the Matlocks, Robert told his companions that he was not well; by the time they reached his bedroom, he said that he was much worse. Remembering Robert's usual solitary prelecture supper of milk, tea, and an egg, they decided that the impending interview with Khrushchev was more terrifying than a lecture, and resolved to wait until morning to make a final decision about the flight to Gagra. They woke early and found him saying that though he was worse, he would do "what he had come for." By half-past six Robert and Frank Reeve were on the way to the airport with Alexei Surkov, Secretary of the Writers' Union, and his translator, Myshkov. It was noon when they reached the Guest House of the Georgian Ministry of Health, a twenty-minute drive from the Premier's dacha. Robert immediately lay down, dozed, and refused all food, asking for perry, a drink made of pear juice and soda, familiar to him since his English days at Dymock in 1912. When Robert said that he could go no farther, Frank Reeve informed Surkov of the state of things and asked for a doctor. Within fifteen minutes a young woman, doctor's bag in hand, appeared at the Guest House. She found nothing worse than indigestion and acute fatigue. Meanwhile Surkov reported that Khrushchev would come to see Robert, bringing his personal physician. After examining the patient, Khrushchev's doctor declared that Robert was well enough to receive the Premier.

Robert quickly put on his shoes and socks and sat up on his bed. Chairs were brought in for Khrushchev and Surkov; the translators took position, each on a bed. Khrushchev's secretary and the host of the Guest House found other seats. After exchanging pleasantries, Robert and the Premier launched into their real talk. There is no substitute for Frank Reeve's report in detail of this dramatic encounter. Robert chiefly tried to urge on Khrushchev that relations between the United States and the Soviet Union should be based on rivalry carried out on the highest possible plane. "We're laid out for rivalry in sports, science,

"Your emblems are the hammer and sickle; mine are the axe and the scythe."

—R.F. to Khrushchev

R.F. at the Café Aelita with Voznesensky (standing) Smith, Reeve, Yevtushenko, Romanova, Mezhelaitis, Adams and Matlock.

(Ja. Brilliant)

112

113

R.F. walks
with the
Honorable
Stewart Udall
at Dumbarton
Oaks, in
Washington,
D.C.

(National Capitol
Parks Service)

art, democracy," Robert said as Reeve quotes him. "That's the real test, which democracy's going to win." After they had run over with remarkable frankness the chief current political agitations, including the touchy subject of Berlin, Khrushchev said to Robert, "You have the soul of a poet." When the Premier had taken his leave, Reeve reports that Robert showed his fatigue "by dropping back on his bed." He had enough elation left to say characteristically, "Well, we did it, didn't we? He's a great man," he went on, "he knows what power is and isn't afraid to take hold of it."

After his return to America, Robert began a letter to Norman Thomas, whom he had known for many years and who had six times been nominated for the presidency by the Socialist Party. Robert's final illness prevented his finishing the letter; the incomplete draft remains in the Baker Library at Dartmouth College. It sums up the hope with which he embarked on his Russian visit. He wanted to tell Khrushchev in person "we shouldn't come to blows till we were sure

"I yield to no one in my admiration for the kind of liberal you have been, you and Henry Wallace. One of the great moments in my life was when we three foregathered at Larry Spivak's party and I stood between you and Henry for a chance photographer to take one picture. . . . I had put my hand on Henry's shoulder in affectionate sympathy. Then you came along and there we three stood in a row against the world. I treasure the picture."
(From a letter to Norman Thomas, September 28, 1962, written but never mailed)

(Robert Striar)

"Except for the time Thomas Jefferson dined here alone, never has there been such a collection of great minds in one room in the White House."
—President Kennedy's opening remarks at the dinner honoring Nobel Prize winners.

(General Services Administration, National Archives and Records Service) there was a big issue remaining between us, of his kind of democracy versus our kind of democracy, approximating each other as they are, his by easing downward toward socialism from the severity of its original ideals, ours by straining upward toward socialism through various phases of welfare state-ism. I said the arena is set between us for a rivalry of perhaps a hundred years. Let's hope we can take it out in sports, science, art, business and politics before ever we have to take it out in the bloody politics of war. It was all magnanimity — Aristotle's great word."

Robert's actual return to this country led to an understandable but unhappy blunder. He was to fly from Moscow with his two companions and Stewart Udall on Sunday, the ninth of September. At the Homer Noble Farm in Vermont, I was alerted by the State Department to make ready for his return. I knew that in addition to age, fatigue, and sickness he would be suffering from almost eighteen hours of virtual sleeplessness. I asked what preparation had been made to protect him from the horde of reporters who would be waiting. The answer: none at all; it was Sunday and all offices would be closed. Restraining my emotions at this news, I called Alfred Edwards, who promised that he would be at the airport and would try to arrange for Robert a private exit from the plane. Despite his careful plans he was blocked and Robert came down the gangplank on the arm of Stewart Udall, looking more dead than alive, and immediately faced a barrage of questions. In his state of let-down and exhaustion, he began to repeat himself, and then astonished Udall by blurting out a version of one of his own often repeated jibes and attributing it to Khrushchev. As reported by Udall, Robert told the reporters: "Khrushchev said he feared for us because of our lot of liberals. He thought that we're too liberal to fight — he thinks we will sit on one hand and then on the other."

Next morning the *Washington Post* carried a headline: Frost says Khrushchev sees the U.S. as "Too liberal to defend itself." By thus putting words into Khrushchev's mouth, Robert seriously embarrassed President Kennedy at the most critical stage of the Cuban missile crisis, and created a tragic breach in his friendship with the President. Some of the steps that had marked the genuineness of this friendship were the President's invitation to Robert to take part in his inaugural, his reception of Robert in private at the White House, the presentation to Robert of the gold medal voted him by Congress, and the inclusion of Robert at a dinner for recipients of the Nobel Prize, the supreme trophy which Robert had coveted but which had escaped him. Not until after Robert's death, at the dedication of the Robert Frost Library at Amherst, did the President, in one of his most eloquent speeches, pay tribute in retrospect to a relation thus unhappily interrupted.

V

On the Highest Plane

Who have, as I suppose, ahead
The darkest of it still to dread.

"Quarrelsome? Certainly—and not with men alone but gods. Tangled in misery? More than most men. But despairing? No. Defeated by the certainty of death? Never defeated. Frightened of the dreadful wood? Not frightened either. A rebellious, brave, magnificent far-wandering old man who made his finest music out of manhood and met the Furies on their own dark ground."

—Archibald MacLeish speaking at the Presidential Convocation and Ground Breaking for the Robert Frost Library at Amherst on October 26, 1963.

Robert's calendar for the month of November 1962 contains a record of perhaps the most active four weeks in his career. As I look back at it, I wonder why we accepted so many engagements. Would the outcome have been different if he had remained quietly at home—aware of his failing health and his eighty-eight years—but chafing at his inability to go where he wanted? Early in the month he paid a visit to Yale, an annual commitment, and from there he went to New York to receive the Edward MacDowell Medal. Four days later he was off again to be given the honorary degree of L.H.D. from the University of Detroit, and from there he went on to Chicago to commemorate the fiftieth anniversary of *Poetry Magazine.* After a public lecture in Greenwich, he spent Thanksgiving in Connecticut at a family gathering. His next visit was to Dartmouth College, where he delivered one of his finest lectures, one on the virtues of extravagance. On Thursday, the twenty-ninth, I traveled with him to New York, where he was to speak at a benefit dinner for the National Cultural Center, which had its headquarters in Washington. Signs that all was not well with him appeared during this New York journey. As we rode the escalator to the upper level in Grand Central Station, where we were to be met by a former Amherst student who had become a doctor, Robert turned to me as I stood one step below him and said: "Brace yourself. I feel faint." But he regained his balance, and when we reached the top he greeted his friend as if nothing had occurred to disturb him. They carried on a conversation that seemed to have been only briefly interrupted since their earlier years at Amherst. I alerted the doctor to Robert's possibly unstable condition, asked him to keep watch in case his services might be called for, and then perhaps to join Robert for dinner at the Carlyle Hotel. Meanwhile I went to the Cosmopolitan Club and waited by the telephone. An hour or so later I received a call reporting that although Robert seemed tired and not at his best, it would be unnecessary and unkind to cancel his talk, to which so many had looked forward. The evening, from Robert's point of view, was not a success. True to form, he blamed himself rather than a program that included too many dissimilar performers and was not designed to give him any ease in his role.

On Friday we took the five o'clock train back to Boston. Robert was still tired but in good spirits. Ted met us at Back Bay and drove us to Robert's house on Brewster Street in Cambridge. We were reluctant to leave him alone as he seemed tired and lonely, but he insisted that he would be all right. On reaching home I alerted Erastus Hewitt, Robert's neighbor, lawyer, and close friend, a man devoted to him and without whose presence on Brewster Street my constant anxieties and concerns would have been much greater.

The next morning I went over to number 35 as usual and found Robert rested and cheerful. We spent the morning catching up with the mail, making plans for the month ahead, and concluding arrangements for his talk before the Ford Hall Forum in Boston the following evening.

On returning home at noon I found bad news. Stafford Dragon had called to tell of the death of his son, Richard, in an automobile accident that morning. Ted and I had known Richard well as a childhood friend of our own children, Anne and Bobby, and we realized that we must be with the Dragon family at some time during the days following. Anne and I promised to be at Ripton by late Monday afternoon; Ted and Anne's husband would follow on Tuesday morning in time for the funeral. I returned to Brewster Street to inform Robert of the accident and to help him with the telephone call I knew he would want to make. Difficult as it was, he made the call, and from the memories of his own losses spoke to Stafford as an equal in grief. After a walk and tea together, I left with the promise to be on hand early Monday morning to take him to the Peter Bent Brigham Hospital, where he had an appointment with the urologist Dr. Hartwell Harrison, who had seen him the month previous and wished to make a further examination.

Sunday passed normally. Before leaving for Brewster Street on Monday morning, I telephoned Robert to be sure he was awake. He replied that he was very sick and couldn't possibly go out. On calling Dr. Roger Hickler, his personal physician, I was told he was out of town but had left as his relief Dr. James Jackson, whom I knew but who had not been introduced to Robert. Dr. Jackson agreed to meet me on the porch at Brewster Street to make plans and form a united front. I knew that Robert would not allow a nurse to attend him even if I could find one at such short notice. It was obviously out of the question to leave him alone in the house. We decided that the only solution was to take him to the hospital for the tests he was scheduled to undergo. The problem was not only to get him there, but to get him there before two o'clock, my deadline for starting with Anne for Vermont.

Our campaign outlined, Dr. Jackson and I went into the house. Leaving the doctor downstairs in the sitting room, I went up to confess to Robert my bold action in summoning medical help. To my surprise he showed none of the resentment I had anticipated; in fact he appeared rather relieved. I suggested that he go downstairs for a talk with the doctor and that meanwhile I would work on some letters in the study. I went to my desk, accomplishing nothing, nervously listening to the rise and fall of tones as voices drifted upstairs. After almost half an hour without a summons I decided to go down and see how matters had progressed. Dr. Jackson stood holding in his hands an assortment of bottles containing pills that had been previously prescribed for Robert, who sat firmly in his chair, hair rumpled and expression angry.

"Dr. Jackson wants to take me to the hospital," he said, turning on me all the pent-up fury he had been too polite to vent on the doctor. I looked at the somewhat startled man who had made the suggestion, hoping that he would fill me in on what had passed between them. He did, but to no avail in reconciling Robert to the idea of hospitalization. I tried reason, explaining to Robert the impossibility of leaving him alone in the house when I had to go to Vermont and represent him at the service for Richard Dragon. No response. I tried again, telling him that if he were in the hospital, it would be much easier for Dr. Harrison to make the necessary tests. That remark sparked the explosion. Robert rose, drawing his red silk wrapper about him like a Roman senator, stood glaring at us both, and announced, "This is when I walk out of your lives—all of you." And with the steely-cold look that he could bring to his eyes, he marched upstairs. Dr. Jackson, somewhat taken aback, quickly explained that from his observation of symptoms and recognition of the pills already prescribed, he considered Robert to be in serious condition and in dire need of hospitalization. This opinion hardly came as a surprise, for I had been warned even before Robert's Russian visit that an emergency might occur at any time, caused by prostate trouble and a possible growth.

"What shall I do?" Dr. Jackson asked, adding, "I'd like to say goodbye to him before I leave." I told him that he would find Robert in the bedroom directly overhead. Dr. Jackson had hardly gone up the stairs before he was down again. Robert had refused to acknowledge his presence. "Was he lying face down or face up?" I asked. "Face down." "In that case," I said, "it will be three hours before I can get him to the hospital. I wish it had been the other way."

I decided not to brave the lion for a while, but to go home briefly to prepare for the drive to Vermont. I was somewhat afraid that on my return to Brewster Street I might find the house barred against me. Not so. I went in to discover Robert in the kitchen eating his much-delayed breakfast of milk, coffee, and raw egg. He asked me to help him pack, to arrange with Dr. Jackson for a pleasant room, and to drive him to the Peter Bent Brigham in Brookline.

As I left him in his hospital room, he said, obviously penitent and aware of the eventualities he might have to face, "I will do this on the highest plane—don't fear."

On my return to Cambridge from Vermont, a severe cold kept me for several days from visiting the hospital. When I was finally declared free from infection, I went the Peter Bent Brigham and found Robert vastly improved in physical condition and somewhat reconciled to the fact that if he wanted to finish what he hoped to accomplish, and as he used to say "to see how it will all turn out," it might be necessary to let the doctors evaluate his state and make their own decisions. Hitherto the medical reports had been inconclusive, but on Saturday Dr. Harrison decided that surgery was the only answer to Robert's condition, and he made plans to operate on the morning of Monday, December tenth.

The only room the hospital had been able to provide when Robert appeared, so suddenly without advance notice, was a small cubicle adjacent to a busy corridor. Aware that Robert might face a long stay in the hospital, I set about making plans for his comfort. In my twenty-four years of service, I had not only heard but learned from experience that Robert was far from the perfect patient. In November 1939 he had spent some ten days at our house in Cambridge suffering from a bad attack of cystitis. It took two nurses, our housekeeper, and all my efforts to maintain a reasonable household equilibrium. Through the foresight and skillful planning of Alfred C. Edwards, Robert's publisher and friend, all necessary financial provision had been made for his comfort and freedom from worry in case of illness. I had, therefore, a virtually free hand in trying to secure suitable quarters for him. With the aid of hospital staff, I found available on the third floor a room that had been occupied by none other than King Ibn Saud of Saudi Arabia when he arrived with his retinue for an eye operation. It was a large room, with windows overlooking the main hospital driveway. It had a fireplace and an adjoining bathroom. It offered space in which to move about and at the same time a kind of peaceful seclusion, situated as it was at the butt end of a corridor. I took it, and engaged nurses for round-the-clock duty, so that Robert could be spared the petty inconveniences and annoyances that I feared would prove a greater trial to him than the actual operation he was to undergo.

Seldom has a man been so fortunate as Robert in the doctors who attended him. An old friend, Dr. George Thorn, was Physician-in-Chief at the Brigham. Dr. Hartwell Harrison, who performed the first operation, and Dr. Francis Moore, who did the second, were warm, friendly men with intellectual interests that tallied with Robert's own. His personal physician, Dr. Roger Hickler, was graced with the devotion of a son and the firmness of a parent — in this case a necessary combination.

Robert came through the first operation in encouraging condition. He found himself established in the new room with a nurse in attendance; and so began a long siege, though no one at the time foresaw its duration. Two fine nurses, Mrs. Earle by day and Miss Colcord from three in the afternoon till eleven at night, were his mainstays. Night duty was a problem. The shortage of nurses became more acute as the holiday season approached. On one occasion the wife of a member of the hospital board volunteered her services, and many energetic people spent hours on the telephone trying to secure help. My daughter Anne and I worked out our own routine for visiting the hospital and keeping Robert from the sulks or from depression. Anne and her husband were living nearby in Cambridge, so that we could set out together in the morning, bringing mail from Brewster Street, messages from solicitous friends, and the necessary changes of clothing. One sartorial improvement was urged by Gabriel, the colorful Brigham barber, who insisted that Robert's pajama tops be the same blue as his eyes.

When it became obvious that Robert was losing interest in his hospital lunch tray, we formed the custom of stopping on our way to town at Welsh's Fish Shop on Charles Street to collect oysters or shrimps packed in ice by the proprietor, who had known Robert as a customer during his days in the apartment on Mt. Vernon Street. Either

Anne or I, but most often both of us, stood guard while Mrs. Earle took her lunch break. Our own lunches became a problem. The hospital cafeteria was crowded and slow, a nearby Italian café did not attract us; we began to carry sandwiches with us to eat in Robert's room. This innocent venture brought on Robert's first outburst. As he lay in bed, his tray in front of him, Anne and I eating our sandwiches, Dr. Thorn and his retinue of house physicians entered the room. Anne and I immediately left and waited outside on a corridor bench. When we came back we were met with an icy stare. "I never want you to eat in this room again," Robert broke out. "People will think I am too poor to provide my friends with lunch. No more picnics!"

Crises were few, but each with its own distinction. On one occasion when his daughter Lesley was visiting, I arrived triumphant with a very special lily I had found to cheer him. "Take it away! Don't mock me!" he shouted. I left the room. "What did he mean?" Lesley later asked. I told her that he was asking himself whether he would see another spring. But his wit and play were as evident as his moments of sharpness or rebellion. On a later day, a day of medical crisis of which Robert was unaware, Dr. Thorn came into the room alone and unannounced. Robert noticed the absence of the usual retinue, and asked, "Oh, traveling light?" Perhaps his worst moment occurred when he woke from threatening dreams in the early hours of an uncomfortable morning and saw Oriental faces peering at him. Fearful that he actually was in a foreign country and surrounded by what he called "Asiatics," he tugged at the bell that summoned the head nurse. It took time and patience to explain to him that what he really saw were two of his friends, the Korean head resident and the utterly charming Chinese corridor nurse. His startled vision as he woke may well have thrown him back abruptly to his boyhood in San Francisco, where he and his contemporaries were not discouraged from looking on Chinese immigrants and their children as legitimate targets of abuse, with the result, no doubt that they became also objects of fear—the fear of the unknown, the unfamiliar, or the different. Robert was capable at times of attitudes that today would be called racist, a charge easy to make and almost impossible to rebut. Yet these attitudes mellowed rather than hardened with age, and over the years he found friends among a comprehensive range of persons, priest and rabbi, black and white, Oriental as well as European or American.

Robert's dream-ridden night may have presaged another crisis, this one physical and not emotional. His heart weakened, and signs of clotting appeared. After consultation, Dr. Harrison decided that a second operation would be necessary, a ligature to prevent clots from traveling to vital regions. Again Robert responded well to surgery. His condition seemed to reach an even higher plateau. He received many visitors, too many to list, but each significant in his life: college presidents, Amherst friends, Dartmouth friends, Washington friends, a bishop from Ohio, a railway porter (Jim Canaday) who had not only

On the Highest Plane

In winter in the woods alone
Against the trees I go.
I mark a maple for my own
And lay the maple low.

At four o'clock I shouldered axe
And in the afterglow
I link a line of shadowy tracks
Across the tinted snow.

I see for Nature no defeat
In one tree's overthrow
Or for myself in my retreat
For yet another blow.

Robert Frost

Published
in the volume
In the Clearing
in 1962,
this is
the
last poem by R.F.
to find a place in
his definitive
canon.
(Eric Schaal,
Life Magazine
© Time Inc.)

often helped Robert at the Back Bay Station in Boston but had carried on philosophical discussions while waiting to put him on the train. In 1961 after Robert had recovered from pneumonia in Florida, Jim went to New York to meet the Miami train and escorted him safely back to Brewster Street. Robert's old and devoted friend Louis Untermeyer and his newer friend Stewart Udall, then Secretary of the Interior, called at the Brigham. His publisher, Alfred Edwards, visited frequently. His daughter Lesley, her two girls Elinor and Lee, his grandson, Prescott Frost, and his granddaughter, Robin Hudnut, were in constant communication. A Christmas tree stood in one corner of his room. A watercolor sketch from his anaesthetist, Dr. Vandam, hung on his door, and on the mantelpiece stood an Eskimo carved owl much admired by Robert and, though a cherished possession, loaned him by the Reginald Cooks of Middlebury College.

Meanwhile, advised by the doctors, I had found a couple, Rita and Stuart MacPherson, new arrivals from Prince Edward Island, and had installed them in the Brewster Street house to make ready for Robert's discharge from the hospital. I found a carpenter ingenious enough to turn Robert's old-fashioned bathroom into what he longed for, a room with a modern shower, and had a splinter-free floor laid in his bedroom. Events at the hospital seemed to favor the expectations on which these plans were based.

On the first of January, Franklin Reeve, Robert's interpreter and companion during his Russian visit some four months earlier, came to the hospital with presents — flowers, a calendar drawn and illustrated by his children, and a bottle of champagne. Together he and Robert toasted the New Year and reminisced, recalling the events of their ten days in Russia. As they went on exchanging memories, Reeve reports, Robert "kept talking about wanting to go back to Russia, about getting well again and going over to see Khrushchev for one more conversation, one more talk to straighten things out." Reeve adds: "He'd been writing poetry but he said it was no good. He was close to giving up, he said . . ." a phrase Reeve interpreted to mean dying.

The days following Reeve's visit went smoothly enough. Robert dictated letters, two especially notable, one to G. Roy Elliott and one, the best of all, to Lesley. Both are printed in Lawrance Thompson's *Selected Letters*. The award of the Bollingen Prize on January fifth roused him to renewed activity. He asked Anne and me to bring him delicacies that could be stored in the hall refrigerator so that he could reward the house doctors, whose nightly visits had begun to resemble the soirées he had held regularly at Brewster Street late in the evening after a public lecture. He enjoyed his callers, but the flowers that came every afternoon passed somewhat unnoticed after his first eager look to see the name of the sender. The curiosity of the nursing staff to learn whether anything had come from the President was almost insatiable, but no flowers or message from that quarter arrived to soothe Robert's unspoken disappointment.

On his bedside table stood a five-dollar Baby Ben alarm clock brought from Brewster Street, although he used it there only when he needed to be awakened in order to keep an engagement. Robert, and Lesley too, had an uncanny sense of sun time and relied little on watches or clocks. I noticed that he began to fix his eyes on the dial of the Baby Ben, almost as if watching the hands go round, measuring the hours left to him. Suddenly he would rouse himself from such concentration and take charge of whatever situation was going on around him. He began to be fretful with the nurses and often asked me to explain to them that he did not care to have his hand held, that he did not like anyone sitting on the edge of his bed, and that he did not appreciate badinage about any of the discomforts of his illness. I realized that he began to make more frequent use of the oxygen tube. But in spite of these disturbing symptoms, all of us who were concerned carried on, perhaps unrealistically, with the assumption that he would return to Brewster Street. His mood was such that he might be living out the words he had spoken during his last interview with the press some six weeks earlier: "Money and fame don't impress me much. About all that impresses me is human kindness and warm relationships with good friends. . . . I guess I don't take life very seriously. It's hard to get into this world and hard to get out of it. And what's in between doesn't make much sense. . . ."

By the seventeenth of the month, plans had been completed for Robert to receive a delegation of Russian writers visiting this country under the auspices of the Cultural Exchange Agreement. They were Valentin P. Katayev, novelist, playwright, and editor; Viktor S. Rozov, playwright and author of the widely shown film *The Cranes Are Flying;* and Freda Lurie, described in State Department announcements as consultant on American literature. Freda Lurie and Elena Romanova had interpreted for Robert and Fred Adams when they were in Russia, and had shepherded them about. The two women earned for themselves the title of "the pendragons" for their constant vigilance over their American visitors. Robert had enjoyed meeting both Katayev and Rozov and looked forward to seeing them again. On the agreed date, the afternoon of January twenty-second, the Russians appeared at the hospital, accompanied by Miss Tatiana Kudrjavcev, escort officer and interpreter from our State Department; Mrs. E. Power Biggs from the office of the Harvard University Marshal; and Mrs. Harry Levin, wife of Professor Harry Levin of Harvard and herself Russian. The delegation came bearing flowers, caviar, a doll from the Ukraine, and a folk-art bowl and spoon. After an exchange of greetings, we poured champagne. Robert, propping himself on his elbow and holding his glass, proposed the first toast: "To all comrades Russian and American." In return the Russians replied: "To your good health! To Robert Frost." Katayev and Rozov told Robert of the hard-cover translation of a collection of his poems to be published in the spring and said that a copy of it would be brought to him by Alexander Tvardovski, editor of the literary magazine *Novy Mir.* Tvardovski had been chosen to visit America as Robert's counterpart in the cultural exchange program that took Robert to Russia, but, as it turned out, he never came. The decision as to whether to complete the exchange may not have been Tvardovski's to make.

The visit over, the delegation went immediately to a press interview in another room in the hospital. Katayev was reported as saying, "I am happy to hold the hand of a genius and wonderful man. If all humanity had men like Frost there would be no wars. Life would be different." Although Katayev did not speak these words in Robert's presence, someone may well have reported them, for Robert is said to have made a characteristic riposte: "Men are men. I'm not always so hopeful. War has its rules. We must not cut down apple trees. We must not poison wells."

As I look back on that afternoon with the Russians, two of Robert's comments come to mind. Ill as he was, he still could make a quick rejoinder. When the discussion turned to religion, Robert said: "The religion of Russia is Christian atheism." And on growing old he observed: "When you're young you keep talking about what you're going to do when you grow up. But when you get older, you understand that the most important thing is to be a good human being. One of the best things in the world is just to be good natured." This was a course of thinking that had showed itself in his last press conference in November, and a considerably far cry from his proclamation in 1938: "I'm a bad bad man."

Almost immediately after the visit of the Russian writers, although in no way as a result of it, Robert began to fail in minor but noticeable ways. Worried, I decided to waylay Dr. Thorn as he came out of Robert's room after his daily morning visit. Waiting in the hall, before my arrival had been announced to Robert, I was surprised to see both Dr. Thorn and Dr. Hickler emerge from the room. "We were about to send for you," Dr. Thorn said. He then told me that he and Dr. Hickler during the last two days had made a serious appraisal of Robert's condition and wanted to make plans with me. They wanted me to know that I should give up hope of seeing Robert back in Brewster Street, that therefore it would be wise to plan differently for the MacPhersons. Dr. Hickler, who was my own physician, then said, "You are very tired. I want you to go away for a few days and come back strengthened for some hard weeks ahead." I admitted extreme fatigue and, after consultation with Anne, agreed to go on Saturday, the twenty-sixth, but no farther than to the Whale Inn, recommended by friends, in Goshen, Massachusetts, slightly northwest of Amherst and about three hours' drive from Cambridge. The year had been a hard one, with Robert's Russian trip, Washington duties, the making of the film *A Lover's Quarrel,* and Robert's increasing fatigue and irascibility. My problems did not lie in dealing with him, but in my role as mediator between him, his family, and his friends. I could understand his sudden and unexpected refusals to admit those who wanted to see him, but it was a different matter to explain to the disappointed or the piqued. Anne had promised to take over at the hospital, and to plan in particular for an expected visit, on Sunday the twenty-seventh, which proved to be Robert's last from anyone outside his immediate circle. This was a call from Ezra Pound's daughter, the Countess Mary de Rachewiltz, a call that brought together Robert's early success in England and this country with his last days in the Brigham Hospital and that represented a kind of final reconciliation of his contradictory emotions toward Ezra Pound.

Anne kept rough notes of this interview. She reports the Countess as saying, "I've come to thank you," and adding that it was high time some member of her family expressed thanks. "He'll be glad to know you consented to see me." According to the notes, Robert answered—somewhat equivocally, one must suppose—"I've never got over those days we had together." The Countess remarked that her father didn't say much when he was released, but she supposed that he and Robert understood each other. Robert replied, "Politics makes too much difference to both of us. Love is all. Romantic love as in stones and poems. I tremble with it. I'd like to see Ezra again." The Countess urged him to come to Venice where her father was living. "We followed your travels last year," she told Robert. "When you get your strength back you must come to us." Robert said, "Perhaps I will. The Plimptons and other young friends of his on the *Paris Review* are friends of mine, too." Robert and the Countess joined in praise of Archibald MacLeish. Robert told her that one of the prized things he had received at Christmas was a word from Pound. "I wish we could see more of each other," he said. The Countess assured him that her father was well and was interesting himself in such activities as going to concerts, and she repeated, "He will be glad I was able to see you." Anne's comment on the scene indicates a change that Robert had undergone. She makes the point that Robert was "freed from a certain kind of reticence" by the fear that he might not again see one or another of the people who had figured in his life, and by "the tradition of last statements." She observes that the problem of reporting him accurately in this mood became peculiarly difficult. The danger lay in making him sound sentimental instead of catching the note of liberation which allowed him to express himself without the ironies of half-mischievous animus that characterized so much of his talk.

While this interview was going on, Ted and I were driving toward the Whale Inn at Goshen for my prescribed rest. It proved to be a brief one. Goshen was a snowbound and isolated village, and the weather was bitingly cold. From the outside the Inn looked charming, but despite the telephone reservation Ted had made, we were told that it was closed. We were somewhat reluctantly admitted on the strength of the reservation and shown to a beautifully furnished but icy bedroom. The wind whistled through the windows, only partly kept at bay by an open fireplace which we plied lavishly with wood. We saw members of the inn staff only when they served us superlative meals. At night they vanished into remote recesses of the straggling old building, and we were left utterly alone. Thus it happened that when Anne tried to call us by telephone in the small hours of Tuesday morning, no one heard or answered her ring. In the gray light before sunrise we were wakened by noise on the stairs outside our bedroom and the sound of someone calling our name. Ted put on a wrapper and opened the door. A state trooper was standing half way up the stairs, while one of the inn staff looked up from the foot. Because I had so fully accepted the program the doctors had laid out for me, on the assumption that Robert faced a long and troublesome siege in the hospital, my first thought—and Ted's also—was that something had happened to Anne or perhaps to Anne and her husband. But no—Anne had finally reached us through the state police; the trooper had come to tell us that Robert had died in the hospital early that morning. Later we learned that Anne had been with him for a considerable part of Monday. They had a good day together, and Robert even dictated to her the rough beginning fragment of a poem he was working on. During the night his condition worsened. Dr. Hickler was summoned, and was with him when a pulmonary embolism put an end to his long, brilliant, and often tortured life. It was a quiet end, Dr. Hickler told me; no struggle, no final words, only a peaceful subsidence.

Ted and I started for Cambridge as soon as the helpful trooper had the engine of our Ford going for us in the aching cold. We stopped at Amherst to telephone and to acquire a morning paper. The black public print brought home to me the news I had not really digested. Robert was gone. I had been thinking of the problems that would have to be faced, the arrangements that would have to be made. Of course the word had gone out on radio and television as well as through the press. Katayev, Rozov, and Reeve heard it in a bar in New York. When Ted and I reached Cambridge, we found that others had heard it, too. Waiting in our living room, admitted by our household helper, we discovered Robert's publisher, Alfred Edwards, and John Dickey, President of Dartmouth College. They had started immediately for Cambridge to help with the problems I would face in the next few days. They had already summoned members of Robert's family and arranged with the MacPhersons to make the Brewster Street house ready for lodging and meals. They later helped Lesley arrange a small service for family and close friends in Appleton Chapel in the Harvard Yard, a service conducted by Dr. Palfrey Perkins, minister at King's Chapel in Boston and a man whom Robert knew and admired.

On February seventeenth, a public memorial service was held in Johnson Chapel at Amherst College. On this occasion another friend, Bishop Henry Hobson of Ohio, spoke with utmost understanding of Robert's religious views. He referred to "those who accuse Robert Frost of being deficient in religious faith because they confuse a valid faith

132

with theological orthodoxy. The latter he did not have," said the Bishop; "the former he had to a greater degree than almost any man I have ever known." The Bishop went on to discuss a particular complex of thought and feeling to which Robert gave expression many times in his poems, his letters, and his conversation. This is the idea of the acceptable sacrifice accompanied by the fear that the offering of one's best may prove unacceptable after all, a fear that was very real and deep for Robert, under whose formidable intellect and anything but diminutive ego lurked an insecurity and a humility not always recognized. To me among others he spoke often of the urgency this composite of thought and feeling had for him, and he even charged me with making it clear to any who might not understand. The charge is best carried out through Robert's own words. Of many possible examples, I choose only two. In a letter to Lawrance Thompson in 1948 Robert wrote: "I doubt if I was ever religious in your sense of the word. I never prayed except formally and politely with the Lord's prayer in public. I used to try to get up plausible theories about prayer like Emerson. My latest is that it might be an expression of the hope I have that my offering of verse on the altar may be acceptable in His sight Whoever He is." And finally, in the next to the last speech in *A Masque of Mercy*, Robert gives to the character he names Paul the following lines:

> We have to stay afraid deep in our souls
> Our sacrifice—the best we have to offer,
> And not our worst nor second best, our best,
> Our very best, our lives laid down like Jonah's,
> Our lives laid down in war and peace—may not
> Be found acceptable in Heaven's sight.
> And that they may be is the only prayer
> Worth praying. May my sacrifice
> Be found acceptable in Heaven's sight.

A Note on the Book

This book is set in Linofilm Palatino.
Designed by the German typographer, Hermann Zapf,
Palatino was named after Giovanbattista Palatino,
writing master of Renaissance Italy. It was the first of
Zapf's faces to be introduced to America. The first
designs were cut in 1948, and the casting of the fonts
completed between 1950 and 1952. The book was composed by Ruttle, Shaw & Wetherill, Inc., and printed
by The Murray Printing Company on Warren's Lustro
Offset Enamel, Dull-Ivory, 70# basis, and bound by
Haddon Bindery, Inc.

Jacket, binding, and typography designed by Robert Reed.
Editorial supervision by Louise Waller.
Production supervised by James Lepper.